AF616686

Famous Fighter Squadrons of the RAF

Volume 1

by James J. Halley

Illustrations by Thomas Brittain   Terence Hadler   Michael Trim   Derek Johnson
General Editor Charles W. Cain

Hylton Lacy Publishers Limited, Windsor, England

Series Editor: Charles W. Cain

First published in England, 1971
by Hylton Lacy Publishers Limited,
Coburg House, Sheet Street, Windsor,
Berkshire, England

First Edition 1971
SBN 85064 100 4

Available in the same series

(Of World War Two)

American Fighters	Volume I
German Air Force Fighters	Volume I
Royal Air Force Bombers	Volume I
German Air Force Bombers	Volume I
Royal Air Force Fighters	Volume I
Japanese Navy Bombers	
German Air Force Fighters	Volume II
Royal Air Force Bombers	Volume II
German Air Force Bombers	Volume II
American Fighters	Volume II
French Fighters	
American Bombers	Volume I

Printed in England by Chichester Press Ltd, Chichester, Sussex

Foreword

In recent years there have been many books describing the types of aircraft engaged in two World Wars and a score of smaller conflicts. There have also been many accounts of the careers and adventures of individuals, mainly pilots, who flew these aircraft with outstanding success. However, neither individual skill nor outstanding aircraft can, by themselves, win a war. What is required is team-work and in the Royal Air Force the finest example of this is to be seen in its squadrons.

R.A.F. squadrons are fortunate in having continuity. From the very first day of the Royal Flying Corps, squadrons have retained their identity in contrast to the changes of numbering and nomenclature that have affected the fighting units of other forces. No squadron has avoided disbandment at some time in its history but the traditions of each squadron have lived on in its successors and the crew rooms of today are filled with reminders of past achievements.

In this volume of a continuing series, five squadrons have been chosen from hundreds which have served well the British Commonwealth for sixty years. All five have histories which could fill a book on each so the narratives herein have been restricted by the space available. Certain periods in the careers of these squadrons have been treated more fully than others. They were not chosen on grounds of historical importance but because they were events not shared by the other squadrons. For this reason, No. 111 Squadron's activities in the Middle East during the First World War are allotted more space than its part in the Battle of Britain and the same applies to No. 54 Squadron's sojourn in Australia which was unique, if not particularly vital to the defeat of the enemy.

All five of the squadrons are currently serving, three with Lightnings, one with Phantoms and one with the incomparable vertical take-off Harrier. In each case, their beginnings go back to wood and fabric aircraft whose pilots expended most of their skill and effort in getting them into the air and back to earth again in one piece. As aircraft became more complicated, both air and ground crews learned to operate their heavier and faster mounts, absorbing new methods of coping with the requirements of armament, radio, radar and tactics. In every squadron, the men who flew the fighters depended on the skill and application of its ground personnel. Together they formed a compact and effective unit—the Squadron.

For their assistance in the compilation of this volume we would like to express our gratitude to the ever-helpful staff of the Air Historical Branch, Ministry of Defence, the Public Record Office and the Imperial War Museum. For their aid in illustrating the squadron histories, we thank the contributors of photographs, notably the photographic libraries of the Ministry of Defence, Imperial War Museum and *Flight International.* Our thanks are also due both to Norman Wiltshire of Air-Britain (The International Association of Aviation Historians) and the International Plastic Modellers Society for help with the colour schemes carried by squadron aircraft.

We would also record our appreciation of the courtesy and assistance extended by members of the squadrons in correspondence and during visits; to Wing Commander Ken Hayr of No. 1 Squadron and Flight Lieutenant Mike Shaw (whose own history of No. 1 Squadron is to be published in the near future); for No. 23 Squadron, Wing Commander R. D. Stone and Michael Gething, Esq; for No. 29 Squadron, Wing Commander Brian Carroll and Flight Lieutenant Paul Cooper; for No. 54 Squadron, Wing Commander Ray Bannard and Flight Lieutenant Dick Northcote and for No. 111 Squadron, Wing Commander Peter Collins.

JAMES J. HALLEY
Shepperton, Middlesex, England
August 1971

A NOTE ON SOURCES

The basic information for each squadron has been derived from the Operations Record Books maintained by each unit since 1938 and from earlier records held by the Public Record Office, Where information required for the equipment tables was not available from these, the relevant aircraft movement cards have been analysed. Details of actions are based on combat reports filed at the time and augmented by later information revealed by captured German records. For activities in France in 1939 and 1940 the appropriate A.A.S.F. Intelligence Summaries have been consulted and much background information obtained from squadron scrapbooks and the publications of the Ministry of Defence Information and Public Relations Branches.—J.J.H.

Contents

Colour illustrations

*The illustrations on this page are from copies of the original drawings prepared by The College of Arms. The badges incorporate the crown used at the time the badges were approved for these squadrons, in all cases the King George VI crown. If carried on current aircraft, they would incorporate the Queen's crown. Variations in the interpretation of 'Royal Air Force Blue' will be found on the originals. However, the general concensus of informed opinion suggests that the 'R.A.F. Blue' appearing on No. 23 Squadron's badge is the nearest approximation. The badges are reproduced with the permission of the Ministry of Defence and the Chester Herald (The Inspector of Royal Air Force Badges) and with the kind assistance of the Royal Air Force Club.

No. 1 Squadron: The numeral '1' winged. Motto: *'In omnibus princeps'—'Foremost in everything'.*

No. 23 Squadron: An eagle preying on a falcon. Motto: *'Semper aggressus'—'Always on the attack'.*

No. 29 Squadron: An eagle in flight preying on a buzzard. Motto: *'Impiger et acer'—'Energetic and keen'.*

No. 54 Squadron: A lion rampant semée de Lys. Motto: *'Audax omnia perpeti'—'Boldness to endure everything'.*

No. 111 Squadron: In front of two swords in saltire a cross potent quadrat charged with three seaxes fessewise in pale. Motto: *'Adstantes'—'Standing by'.*

Location of Squadron Bases: United Kingdom and Europe

The following key locates not only the squadron bases but also indicates the period of use.
Note: European Bases are all located in France, unless otherwise stated.

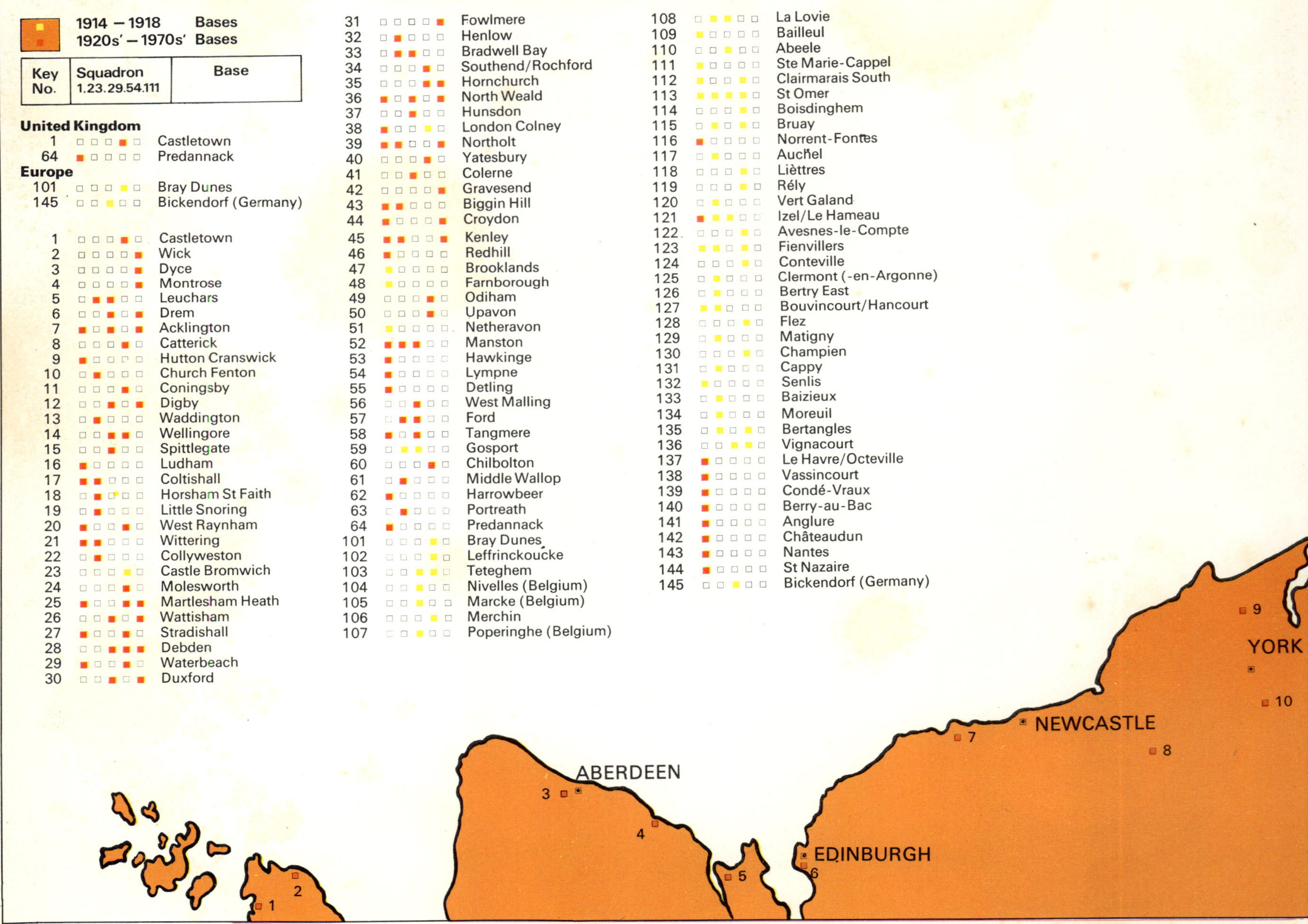

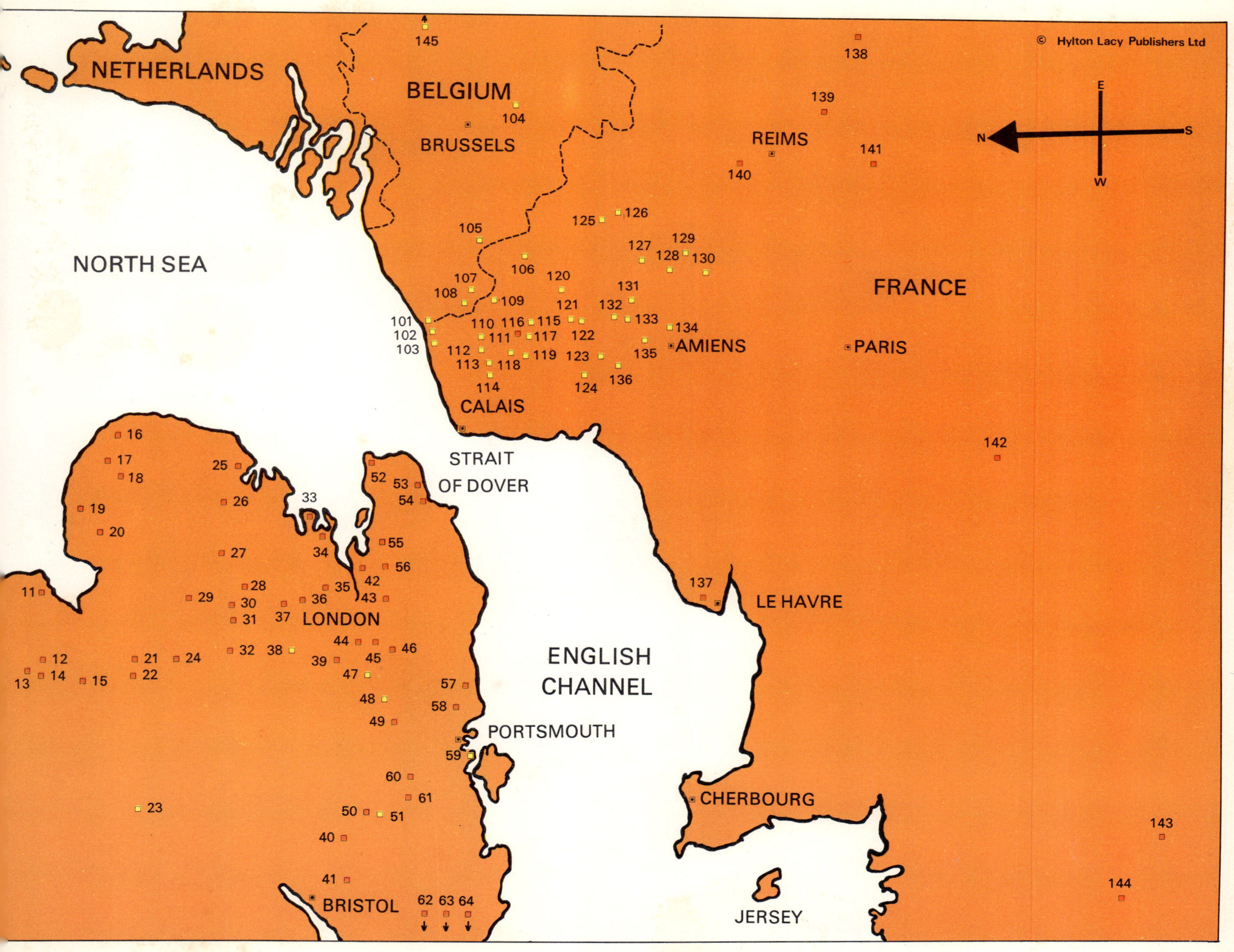
© Hylton Lacy Publishers Ltd
NETHERLANDS
BELGIUM
BRUSSELS
REIMS
NORTH SEA
FRANCE
AMIENS
PARIS
CALAIS
STRAIT
OF DOVER
LONDON
ENGLISH
CHANNEL
LE HAVRE
PORTSMOUTH
CHERBOURG
BRISTOL
JERSEY
N
S
E
W

Squadron Standards

(Left, top to bottom)
The Standards of Nos. 1, 23 and 29 Squadrons, Royal Air Force

(Right, top and bottom)
The Standards of Nos. 54 and 111 Squadrons, Royal Air Force.

(*Above*) No. 23 Squadron, R.A.F. Ceremony on 28 June 1957, when Marshal of the Royal Air Force, Sir John Slessor, GCB, DSO, MC, (Chief of Air Staff 1950-52) visited R.A.F. Station Coltishall to present the Standard to the Squadron in which he had served as a Second Lieutenant, R.F.C.—in 1915.

(*Above, right*); No. 1 Squadron, R.A.F. The Standard of No. 1 Squadron being paraded on 23 June 1958, on the occasion of the relinquishment of R.A.F. Station Tangmere by Fighter Command and the handing over of the Standard to the new No. 1 (ex-No. 263) Squadron. In the background, the old No. 1's Sapphire-powered Hunter F.5s.
(Photos: M.O.D. PRB13504 & 15220)

Royal Air Force Squadron Standards specially photographed in colour by kind permission of the respective Commanding Officers.

(Photos: © Hylton Lacy Publishers Ltd)

No. 1 Squadron

Above One of No. 1 Squadron's first aircraft was 'Beta', a non-rigid airship developed over several years at the Royal Aircraft Factory, Farnborough. The ground handling party makes ready to haul the ship down for mooring. (*Photo: Royal Aeronautical Society.*)

Right 'Gamma' being walked-out for a flight. Evidence of improving techniques can be seen in the swivelling propellers which enabled vertical take-offs to be made. (*Photo: Royal Aeronautical Society.*)

The early days

Having existed for 60 years, No. 1 Squadron is looked upon as the premier fighter squadron of the Royal Air Force. Yet, when it was formed six decades ago fighters had not been thought of—the squadron's first equipment comprised two non-rigid airships.

On 13 May 1912*, the Royal Flying Corps became a physical reality when the Army's No. 1 Airship Company of the Air Battalion, Royal Engineers, was transferred to become the R.F.C.'s No. 1 (Airship and Kite) Squadron. In the process, No. 1 Squadron acquired two small airships named the *Beta* and the *Gamma*. With these lighter-than-air craft, the squadron began to develop its reconnaissance abilities in joint manoeuvres with the Army. Three more followed: the *Delta* in November 1912; the *Zeta* next, a weirdly-shaped Clement-Bayard airship which was destined to be virtually permanently grounded; and, the *Eta* which flew for the first time on 18 August 1913. The following month, on 21 September, the *Eta* was handed over by the Royal Aircraft Factory (Farnborough, Hampshire) and, together with the *Delta*, took part in the 1913 Army manoeuvres in Derbyshire.

These joint manoeuvres provided the R.F.C. with much useful experience. For example, it was discovered during reconnaissance over 'enemy' forces that a brigade of cavalry could possess a marked similarity to a heath dotted with gorse bushes. But many professional soldiers remained sceptical of this innovation; not least the General Staff which was kept informed of the shortcomings of aerial reconnaissance, relying as it did on the uncertain efficiency of the primitive wireless-telegraphy equipment carried by the airships.

* Historically, a special Army Order (February 28, 1911) came into effect on 1 April of that year with the establishment of the Air Battalion, R.E. Similarly, by Royal Warrant (13 April, 1912) the R.F.C. was sanctioned but actually formed as such four weeks later.—Editor.

Flights of up to 5½ hours were made but progress was slow, one 21-mile sortie taking 1 hour 8 minutes. On 1 January 1914, airships were transferred to the Naval Wing but No. 1 Squadron continued to operate at Farnborough until 1 May when it changed its name to the Airship Detachment, R.F.C.

On the same day, No. 1 became a cadre unit only and began to reform at Brooklands when the First World War broke out in August. What miscellaneous aircraft had been acquired were abducted by the other squadrons destined to accompany the British Expeditionary Force to France and No. 1 had to start from scratch. A collection of Bleriots, Farmans and Bristol Boxkites was assembled and in November the squadron moved to Netheravon on the northern fringe of Salisbury Plain where training of the R.F.C. was concentrated.

By March 1915, training was complete and preparations for moving to France began. On 2 March, eight Avro 504s and four B.E.8s flew to Folkestone and on 7 March crossed the Channel to St. Omer to join 3rd Wing. Three days later, No. 1 Squadron made its first war flight.

At that time, reconnaissance was the only task given to aircraft by the Army. Early aircraft with their unreliable engines sputtered slowly over the trench lines sketching enemy positions and occasionally exchanging shots from revolvers and rifles with their opposite numbers in the German air units. This was not to last as both sides began fitting machine-guns and gradually air fighting developed.

On 12 May, the squadron flew its first offensive sortie when four aircraft dropped 20-lb bombs on Don railway junction, Lieutenant O. M. Moullin failing to return, a 'dead' engine resulting in his being taken prisoner.

No. 1 Squadron's first success against enemy aircraft occurred on 5 July 1915, when Captain D. E. Stoddart and Second Lieutenant M. S. Stewart were flying in an Avro (military serial number 4223) near Menin on the Ypres front. At 7,000 feet they encountered an Aviatik and closed with it. The enemy opened fire with a machine-gun from 800 feet above the Avro and for 25 minutes the two aircraft circled, the Avro on the inside turn. Then the Avro's gun jammed and while it was being cleared the Aviatik disappeared to the north. At exactly the same time as this combat ended, an enemy aircraft crashed between Belleghem and Rolleghem; it appears likely that No. 1 had destroyed its first enemy aircraft.

The same Avro (4223) was out again next day flown by Second Lieutenant O. D. Filley with Lieutenant Playfair as observer. An Aviatik was pursued twice near Langemarck before being sighted a third time. On nearing it another Aviatik was seen nearby and over St. Julien shots were exchanged but Playfair's gun jammed. After it had been cleared, only five rounds were left but the Avro returned to the attack. A burst of enemy fire hit it and Playfair was fatally wounded, becoming the squadron's first casualty from enemy aircraft.

By the end of the month 4223 had been patched up and was back in action. When Filley went out on reconnaissance with Second Lieutenant Jacks on 31 July, the Avro was armed with a fixed Lewis gun firing forward and another for the observer. The first enemy aircraft attacked was too fast and made off in a dive; a second approached and when Jacks opened fire it turned away.

Armament for the early fighters was improvised and full of frustrations for the airmen. Lieutenant E. O. Grenfell climbed in the squadron's Bristol Scout single-seater (serial no. 1602) after a Taube seen at 15,000 feet over Houthem. The relatively fast Scout overtook the enemy and at 60 feet he shut off his engine and fired the Lewis gun fixed to the cockpit. Obviously taken by surprise, the observer started to get out his rifle while the pilot nose-dived away. Because of the awkwardly outward-angled mounting of the Lewis necessary to fire clear of the propeller, Grenfell found it difficult to bring his gun to bear on the target without danger of turning into him.

Enemy fighters began to appear in numbers over the front. Fokker E.III single-seat monoplanes made their appearance during the summer of 1915 and its armament of one fixed machine-gun was made infinitely more effective by the adoption of synchronizing gear enabling direct, forward fire through the propeller disc and thus dispensing with awkwardly angled guns.

and most single-seat fighters carried their guns on the top wing out of reach of the pilot. The Lewis had a 47-round magazine which had to be changed by the pilot reaching up from the cockpit, a task not relished by those under attack by the enemy.

The Morane Parasol monoplanes used by No. 1 for reconnaissance also saw their share of action. Second Lieutenants R. Balcombe Brown and T. Hughes were flying Parasol 1894 between Ypres and Courtrai when four Albatros two-seaters attacked. Fire was returned with the front gun while the observer, feeling redundant without a gun, sat pointing his telescope at the enemy to keep them away from the tail until they finally gave up and went home!

Another Parasol manned by Captain R. A. Saunders and Second Lieutenant C. B. Joske attacked an Aviatik over Ypres with a fixed Lewis for the pilot and a Winchester automatic rifle for the observer. During the chase it was joined by two more but was seen to be hit by tracer at 50 yards range. Smoke and flame came from the engine and it dived into woods beyond Passchendaele.

A few Nieuport Scouts had been received and, while flying No. 5171, Captain E. L. Gower found an enemy two-seater near Bailleul. The enemy observer opened up at 1,000 yards and, with an apparently inexhaustible supply of ammunition continued to fire at the Nieuport throughout the action. After expending his meagre 47 rounds, Gower had to retire to change drums and the enemy aircraft departed still spraying bullets. This operational drawback was subsequently resolved, the gun mountings on Scouts being modified to make the gun more accessible.

In January 1917, No. 1 Squadron finally became a fighter unit when it disposed of the last of its reconnaissance-type aircraft and became fully equipped with Nieuport single-seat fighters.

Formation flying became important as a means of bringing a force of fighters into a favourable tactical position and patrols of five or six aircraft became normal. Their purpose was to engage any enemy aircraft attempting reconnaissance flights over the Allied lines and to defend 'friendly' observation aircraft from enemy fighter patrols. Individual combats developed into melées of a dozen or more aircraft gyrating around the sky in attempts to get astern of an enemy.

A typical instance took place on 9 June 1917, when Lieutenant F. Sharpe flying B3481 led a patrol of nine Nieuports over Menin. Three German two-seaters were seen and attacked, attracting the attention of 19 Albatros fighters to the scene. Second Lieutenant Campbell (in B1689) fired a burst into an Albatros at 20 yards range which went down rolling over and over. A second burst into another enemy sent it down with the pilot slumped in the cockpit. While following it down Campbell was attacked by a number of enemy fighters and with his gun jammed succeeded in using the Nieuport's ability to out-climb the enemy. Sharpe had fired at a red-and-green Albatros before having to retire, temporarily, to rectify a gun stoppage. With the gun jam cleared, he picked up two more Nieuports and attacked a Rumpler without apparent effect. Others in the formation fired without result. On the way home, Second Lieutenant Atkins force-landed and overturned in B1522 without injury while Second Lieutenant Mussared was posted missing in B1550. All the pilots had been plagued with trouble from their guns; a theme which was to prevail for as long as Lewis guns were used in remote and inaccessible positions on the aircraft.

Despite the shortcomings of the Nieuport's armament, some pilots were highly successful. Captain Philip F. Fullard, DSO, MC, shot down his first enemy aircraft

1

2

3

4

1 An airship's bulk made some protection from the wind desirable; suitably-angled groves of trees were ideal as improvised docks while operating away from base. (*Photo: Royal Aeronautical Society.*)

2 Major E. M. Maitland, No. 1 Squadron's first Commanding Officer and Captain the Hon C. M. P. Brabazon among a group of army officers visiting 'Gamma' during manoeuvres in August 1913. (*Photo: Royal Aeronautical Society.*)

3 The car of 'Beta' provided more protection for the crew than contemporary heavier-than-air types. Access to the engine in flight was also very useful in an age of temperamental motors. (*Photo: Royal Aeronautical Society.*)

4 A Nieuport of No. 1 Squadron is started-up in the snow at Bailleul in December 1917. The censor has scratched out the aircraft serial but No. 1's identification band is visible on the fuselage above the flight leader's pennant. (*Photo: I.W.M. No. Q11955.*)

on 26 May 1917. When he left No. 1 Squadron at the end of November he had been credited with 19 enemy aircraft confirmed as destroyed, 23 shot down 'out of control' (that is, not seen to crash or catch fire) and three observation balloons.

One of the last actions with Nieuports resulted in the destruction of a Gotha bomber near Neuve Eglise on 12 December 1917. Captain W. W. Rogers (in B6825) saw 17 Gothas flying west at 7,500 feet and led his patrol above them. One of the Gothas left the formation and Rogers closed in and set it on fire. The big bomber broke up and crashed north of Frelinghem where the Army confirmed its destruction.

In January 1918, the Nieuports were replaced by S.E.5as. With a superior top speed of 120 m.p.h. (compared to the Nieuport 17's 107 m.p.h.) the S.E.5a also had better armament. A fixed Vickers machine-gun was mounted on top of the engine forward of the pilot; while a Lewis, fitted to the top wing, could be pulled down to a vertical position on a special Foster mounting. This eased reloading and also enabled the pilot to fire upwards at varying angles.

With the new S.E.5a, No. 1 began a successful period of its wartime career. Now equipped with one of the most effective fighters of the war, the squadron accounted for many enemy aircraft. How effective may be judged by a sortie flown by an American pilot of the squadron on 30 August 1918. Lieutenant Harold A. Kullberg was flying B8427 and escorting D.H.9 bombers near Bourlon when three Fokker D.VIIs—the most potent of German fighters—attacked a straggler. Kullberg dived down on one D.VII and fired a burst from both guns at short range. The enemy fighter pulled up and a wing came off. The other two D.VIIs began to attack from below but Kullberg got on the tail of one and it went down out of control to be seen to crash by another squadron pilot. Then on 16 September, and flying his usual B8427, Kullberg accounted for another D.VII which fell near Valenciennes. But in turn, B8427 was set upon by five more D.VIIs and Kullberg was wounded three times in the leg before escaping at ground level. Three days after being awarded the Distinguished Flying Cross, Lieutenant Kullberg was invalided home; his tally stood at 12 enemy aircraft and one observation balloon destroyed.

On 29 October, Captain R. T. Hoidge MC (in E5799) was flying in company with Lieutenant W. A. Smart (D6973) when he spotted a D.VII harrying an observation balloon. Diving on the enemy, Hoidge managed a brief burst when the Vickers jammed. Clearing the stoppage quickly, he got in another burst, whereupon the Fokker sideslipped and the pilot jumped. The enemy's parachute billowed out—an advantage denied R.F.C./R.A.F. crews in World War One on the now dubious grounds that such safety devices might dilute the 'offensive spirit'. Meanwhile, Hoidge's companion singled out a D.VII from a large formation and closed. Smart saw it go down trailing smoke and another squadron pilot confirmed that it crashed and burst into flames near Landrecies.

Just under two weeks later, the Armistice was agreed and hostilities ceased but it was not before January 1919 that the squadron returned to England—ferrying back nearly 100 S.E.5as in the process—and was reduced to a cadre. Transferred to London Colney (near St. Albans, Hertfordshire), the cadre remained without aircraft until October when it moved to the Royal Air Force Depot at Uxbridge (Middlesex) for disbandment. On 20 January 1920, No. 1 Squadron ceased to exist.

One Squadron in the wilderness

The R.A.F. has never been without a No. 1 Squadron for long and on the day following its demise at Uxbridge, No. 1 reformed at Risalpur on the North-West Frontier of India. Here the Indian Army had been engaged in sporadic warfare with marauding tribesmen for whom the crowded towns of the plains held an irresistible attraction. For centuries the hill tribes had been raiding the villages and towns, a practice which offended against the proprieties of the Victorian soldiers and civil servants whose administration had spread during the 19th century to the remotest corners of the great sub-continent.

For many years, columns of Indian and British troops, aided by bodies of scouts of varying eccentricity, had launched expeditions into the mountains to deter and punish incursions into the peaceful areas. Destruction of crops and houses around a raiding tribe's home villages usually meant a quiet period while the would-be invaders rebuilt their dwellings; permanent occupation was out of the question for the relatively small number of troops involved. Anything which would reduce the requirement for troops was to be welcomed and in 1916 aircraft began to be used. No. 31 Squadron arrived at Risalpur during the first months of 1916 and their B.E.2cs began reconnaissance flights over the mountains. This saved much cavalry patrolling and, after the end of the war, aircraft were regarded as one way in which the cost of maintaining forces in India could be cut. A system of air policing was evolved by which air action could be taken against hostile tribes with economy of force.

There were two main facets of air support and control in disturbed areas. Where troops were in contact with hostile forces, the aircraft provided reconnaissance, communications and air support by attacking enemy positions holding up the ground forces. Acting on their own, they could burn crops and villages by air attack with far less risk of casualties than was involved when a column had to fight its way through mountain passes while being sniped at by tribesmen from the rocks. Casualties were further reduced by the requirement that before any bombing took place the population should be informed. The first stage of any punitive action was for leaflets in the appropriate dialect to be dropped over the offending villages. The population, clutching their most prized possessions, retired to a safe distance until the aircraft had dropped their bombs.

For the most part, D.H.9As and Bristol Fighters carried out these duties but behind the tribal control operations lay a larger requirement. The North-West Frontier had always been seen as a potential invasion route for the Russians. Tsarist dreams of expansion had always been a threat to India for as long as the forces of the British Empire had stood guard. The advent of Bolshevism seemed to offer even less chance of the possibility of invasion waning and the Army had to be prepared for incursions through Afghanistan. An R.A.F fighter squadron for India was authorized and No. 1 began flying Sopwith Snipe single-seaters in 1920. The dusty airfield at Risalpur played havoc with the Snipe's rotary engine and in May the squadron moved to Bangalore in Southern India for a year.

While the Indian Army had been indulging in its traditional activities on the North-West Frontier, a new responsibility had been thrust on the R.A.F. Mesopotamia had been conquered during the war and a new kingdom of Iraq came into being. Having been under Turkish control for centuries, government of the new country was precarious. In the north, troops of a new Turkey led by Kemal Ataturk were active while on the Persian border the Kurds were making life difficult for representatives of the Baghdad government. Various tribes were at each others' throats and the situation was complicated by bands of marauders whose motives were more economic than political.

A system of control similar to that in India was authorized and R.A.F. squadrons began patrols and proscription raids. The veteran D.H.9As and Bristol Fighters were supplemented by two-motor Vickers Vernon and Vimy transports and at the end of April 1921, No. 1 Squadron was ordered to move to Iraq. During May, No. 1 was established at Hinaidi outside Baghdad and next month began flying. It was not until March 1922 that the squadron began to take part in attacks on hostile groups.

Heat and sand did nothing for the life of the Snipe's Bentley rotary and each had to be overhauled after 30 hours flying time. The Aircraft Depot could not keep

1 A Lewis 0·303in machine gun mounted on a Nieuport. As the trigger was almost inaccessible, the gun was fired by means of a Bowden cable from the cockpit. (*Photo: I.W.M. No. Q11957.*)

2 No. 1 Squadron lined up in the snow at Bailleul in December 1917. Individual aircraft identity letters are in use but the style of the markings tended to vary from aircraft to aircraft. Several of the aircraft in this line-up are camouflaged and the censor has obliterated the serial numbers. (*Photo: I.W.M. No. Q11956.*)

3 One of No. 1 Squadron's Nieuports at the end of its fighting career. Passing through Serny airfield while the activities of No. 27 Squadron's D.H.4s were being photographed for the press, B6825 is pressed into service as 'a fighter ready to escort a bomber on a raid'. The date was 17 February 1918 and within a few weeks the Nieuports had been replaced by S.E.5as. (*Photo: I.W.M. No. Q11978.*)

4 Nieuport 27 B6768 shows the camouflage scheme used on No. 1's aircraft and the upward-angled sight for the Lewis gun mounted on the top wing. (*Photo: No. 1 Squadron archives.*)

1

2

up with the demand for overhauled engines and the squadron was always short of flyable aircraft until it formed its own engine overhaul section and took over the work completely.

The tasks allotted included chasing night raiders back into the hills, escorting road convoys (and patrolling the roads on the look out for ambushes), reconnaissance for the police and troops, and message dropping and pick-up. If a village was to be searched for arms and outlaws, the inhabitants were penned in by machine-gun attacks ahead of anybody attempting to break out. If these warnings did not deter, the group could be treated as hostile and attacked. Normally no firing took place until the aircraft was itself fired on and as a result many patches began to appear covering bullet holes. While operating away from base, detachments flew from rough strips near army units and at night pushed their aircraft into 'serais', wood and brush enclosures which protected them from wind and rifle fire. Normally, aircraft operated in pairs so that if one force landed the other could often land and pick up the crew. On one occasion, a Snipe brought home a stranded pilot lying on the wing hanging on to the inner struts. Each aircraft carried a rifle and 150 rounds while each man carried a Service revolver and 50 rounds.

In July 1922, two squadron aircraft were detached to Kirkuk to help pursue a notorious brigand, Kerim Fatteh Beg, responsible for the murder of two officers. After expending 6,360 rounds in the course of several attacks on his band escaping into Kurdistan, No. 1's aircraft accounted for several bandits but the main villain escaped and his name continued to appear on the operations summaries for many years to come.

Despite the presence of aircraft, ground activity continued in the traditional manner. In May 1925, the 2nd Cavalry Regiment of the Iraq Levies was engaged in operations against a large number of rebel tribesmen near Sulaimani. A detachment of Snipes had been sent to co-operate with this force, but on the approach of aircraft the enemy melted into caves and rocks. Between 400 and 500 tribesmen attacked the column which was encumbered with a mass of civilian transport. Using a nullah for cover, the regiment lined the banks under fire from hills full of snipers. Lieutenant Colonel Lawrence, commanding the troops, decided that the only solution was to charge the enemy and chose one hill. The tribesmen retreated in the face of this action and were caught by Flight Lieutenant Luxmoore's fighters on reaching flat ground. Heavy casualties were sustained.

Operating in primitive conditions with old aircraft, it was not surprising that the aircraft attrition was considerable. Fortunately for the British Treasury, the

3-4

5

1 Twelve Snipe of No. 1 Squadron in formation over the Tigris near Baghdad. The aircraft on the extreme left is flown by Pilot Officer D. Boyle, later Marshal of the Royal Air Force Sir Dermot Boyle. (*Photo: Ministry of Defence H.802.*)

2 Forerunner of a long line of squadron photographs of similar layout, but with larger and faster aircraft as background, is this well-known photograph of No. 1 Squadron's personnel and S.E.5as at Clairmarais on 3 July 1918. (*Photo: I.W.M. No. Q.12063.*)

3 Snipe E6939 on the hard-baked sand at Hinaidi, Iraq. The fuselage serial has suffered from the sand thrown up by the wheels on take-off. (*Photo: No. 1 Squadron archives.*)

4 A Nighthawk fitted with a Bristol Jupiter was tested by No. 1 Squadron under tropical conditions. J6926 was a British Nieuport-built aircraft rebuilt by Gloucestershire Aircraft in 1922. (*Photo: Ministry of Defence H.1604.*)

5 One way to keep a Snipe cool was to park it in the shade of a larger aircraft, in this case a Victoria III of No. 70 Squadron. Snipe E8249 carries an individual identification number '3'. (*Photo: Air-Britain archives.*)

bulk of the aircraft used during the 1920s was of wartime origin and of little capital value. But, less satisfactory was the incidence of the pilots and observers facing the hazards of engine failure over hostile territory. Forced landings often meant that the aircraft had to be abandoned as salvage was uneconomic. Serviceable engines and equipment were removed if possible for use with stored airframes.

Only a few days before the squadron disbanded, Pilot Officer F. S. Harricks took off in Snipe H4866 from Kirkuk to bomb a rebel village. When he failed to return, search aircraft set out but found no trace. Later it was found that the aircraft had crashed into a house and was destroyed when its bombs exploded, killing the pilot.

On 1 November 1926, No. 1 Squadron was withdrawn from Iraq Command and its personnel posted to No. 8 Squadron pending distribution among other squadrons in Iraq. Flying Officer G. A. F. Bucknall was the exception. He was posted back to the United Kingdom to form a connecting link with the new No. 1 Squadron to be formed at Tangmere, Sussex, sailing in the liner *Derbyshire* from Basra on 2 January 1927.

No. 1 Squadron in Defence

The task of rebuilding No. 1 (Fighter) Squadron began on 1 February 1927, when Flying Officer Bucknall reported to Tangmere. At first only a cadre was formed and on 21 March, Flight Lieutenant F. L. Luxmoore, DFC, who had served with the squadron in Iraq, arrived to command. As more personnel arrived, the cadre grew and on 1 April the squadron was expanded to a headquarters and one flight with eight officers on strength. Squadron Leader E. D. Atkinson, DFC, AFC assumed command on 11 April and two days later three Siskin III's were delivered so that flying could begin. These Mk. IIIs were followed within a few weeks by Siskin IIIA's which were to be No. 1's equipment for nearly four years.

The Armstrong Whitworth Siskin had started life in 1918 as the Siddeley Siskin but its engine, the A.B.C. Dragonfly had met so many development problems that it prevented any of the aircraft designed around it from entering service. Development continued after the war and fitted with an Armstrong Siddeley Jaguar engine it was adopted by the R.A.F. as a replacement for the wartime Snipe. The Mark III had a mixed wood and metal structure but the Mark IIIA's were all-metal with fabric covering. With an armament of two Vickers machine-guns mounted forward of the cockpit, the Siskin had a maximum speed of 156 m.p.h. and could climb to 15,000 feet in 10½ minutes.

For a year the squadron practised with their new equipment and at the end of May 1928, when it was due to spend a week at the armament training camp at Sutton Bridge (Norfolk) the intensive training paid off. No. 1 Squadron won the trophy presented by Sir Philip Sassoon, the Under Secretary of State for Air, for the best results in gunnery. A few weeks later four Siskins took part in the R.A.F.'s Hendon Air Display.

By 1930, re-equipment of the fighter squadrons was well under way. The Bristol Bulldog had been selected as the standard fighter but the R.A.F. squadrons based on the coast at Tangmere (Sussex) and Hawkinge (Kent) had their eyes on something more potent. The Hawker Hornet had appeared in 1929 and the Air Staff decided to equip a few interceptor squadrons with the type which was renamed 'Fury'. Its higher cost compared to the Bulldog prevented wide adoption and only

Nos. 1, 25 and 43 Squadrons were selected to fly it.

No. 43 Squadron received Furies before No. 1, much to the latter's chagrin. There were suspicions that this unfortunate precedence might be ascribed to the incident whereby No. 1's adjutant had written-off the prototype Hornet in a collision with a 43 Squadron Siskin (over Halnaker, a few miles north of Tangmere, on 11 April 1930) and that this had affected the Air Staff's decision. No. 1's adjutant, Flying Officer Brake, used his parachute and escaped with a broken arm.

Several other Siskins had been lost. On 23 February 1931, Sergeant Ashton had the engine of J8059 cut on take-off and crashed in the adjoining field, fracturing his leg. Then on 6 May, Flying Officer Davys and Sergeant Blake collided over Farnborough (Kent) but both parachuted to safety unhurt.

The squadron's Furies finally arrived in February 1932—after both Nos. 25 and 43 had been equipped—and remained for 6½ years. They were beautiful aircraft with a maximum speed of 207 m.p.h. and the ability to climb to 10,000 feet in 4½ minutes. The armament remained at two Vickers machine-guns. During 1932 radio was installed as standard equipment.

Regular training continued over the years as new tactics and equipment were developed to meet the growing menace of the bomber.

No. 25 Squadron exchanged its Fury Is for improved Fury IIs in December 1936 and passed on five of its old Mk. Is to No. 1 Squadron to bring its strength up to two flights of twelve aircraft each—five being reserve aircraft. In February 1937, No. 1's 'A' Flight was given permission to practise formation aerobatics for the Hendon Display and on 13 April four aircraft flew to Northolt (Middlesex) piloted by Flight Lieutenant E. M. Donaldson, Flying Officer H. E. C. Boxer, and Pilot Officers P. R. Walker and P. P. Hanks. Their display routine was to be demonstrated to the officer in charge of the Hendon Display in competition with teams from Nos. 3 and 54 Squadrons. By the end of the month, the squadron was informed that their team had been selected and during the summer it performed at several air displays. At the end of July, Donaldson led the team to Zurich where they gave three demonstrations at the International Air Meeting. The precision flying of the Furies made a marked impression on the watchers but the German participants gave the British pilots food for thought. Examples of the fast Dornier Do 17 bomber and the sleek Messerschmitt Bf 109 fighter were present. Both were all-metal monoplanes with enclosed cockpits and fully retractable undercarriages; and both considerably faster than the squadron's biplane Furies.

The Royal Air Force had begun to expand at last and, in February 1937, squadron pilots collected eight Gladiator biplanes from the Gloster factory at Hucclecote (Gloucestershire). These were not to re-equip No. 1 but to enable 'B' Flight to be detached to form the nucleus for the newly-reformed No. 72 Squadron, a new 'B' Flight being formed on 5 April.

New equipment came in the following year. On 15 October 1938, three Hurricanes were collected from the Hawker factory aerodrome (then at Brooklands, Surrey) and by 7 November conversion to the new monoplanes was complete. The Munich crisis of a few weeks before had made urgent the task of re-equipping with aircraft capable of meeting German fighters and bombers on equal terms. However pleasant the Fury was to fly, its slow speed and light armament rendered it of little use as an interceptor. The Hurricanes, with a top speed of 322 m.p.h. at 20,000 feet, a similar rate of climb to the Fury and an armament of eight 0.303-in. Browning machine-guns gave R.A.F. pilots an aircraft equal or better to any foreign fighter.

Intensive training kept every section of the squadron busy. The high-powered Rolls-Royce Merlin engine gave the Hurricane a performance which required many changes in flying technique, there being less margin for error than with the handy Furies. Ground staff faced the complexities of hydraulics, new engines and armament. By the time reservists were called up at the end of August 1939, the squadron was ready for action.

Part of the Anglo-French War Plan involved the movement of two forces of R.A.F. aircraft to France on the outbreak of war. An Air Component of fighters and army co-operation aircraft went with the British Expeditionary Force (B.E.F.) while the short-range Fairey Battle light bombers of No. 1 Group moved to fields around Reims—from which they could reach German targets. With the bombers as part of the Advanced Air Striking Force (A.A.S.F.) were to go two fighter squadrons and Nos. 1 and 73 Squadrons had been selected. Forty-two vehicles were collected to make No. 1 mobile and, on 4 September, the ground party left for France. The Hurricanes remained and flew patrols for a few more days until 8 September when the squadron left for Le Havre. Led by Flight Lieutenant 'Johnny' Walker No. 1's pilots taxied out and took off from their home airfield. Their old friends and rivals in No. 43 Squadron wished them 'Good Luck!' over the radio as the camouflaged fighters headed out over the English Channel for France.

France 1939-40

No. 1 Squadron's first airfield in France was the new Le Havre airport at Octeville where next day, 9 September, the commanding officer had everyone digging slit trenches followed by flights over the area

1

2

1 No. 1 Squadron's Furies were a favourite subject for aerial photographers. Individual identification letters were carried on the engine side-panels and spinners were painted in flight colours. (*Photo: Flight International 13392.*)

2 A Siskin IIIA of No. 1 Squadron, J8671, is pegged down for the night. (*Photo: Ministry of Defence H.18.*)

3 The tractability of the Fury gave No. 1 a chance to formate in '1' formation for the benefit of John Yoxall, 'Flight's' chief photographer. (*Photo: Flight International 13390.*)

4 No. 1 Squadron poses for the camera over Sussex in 1933 in three-plane 'vees'. (*Photo: Flight International 12925.*)

5 Siskins being refuelled for the Hendon Air Display in June 1929 from a Morris-Commercial tanker, an early version of the self-propelled 'bowser' that became a familiar sight on RAF airfields. Note the bead sight mounted on the engine and the 'personalised' chocks for each aircraft. (*Photo: Ministry of Defence H.20.*)

3

4

5

1

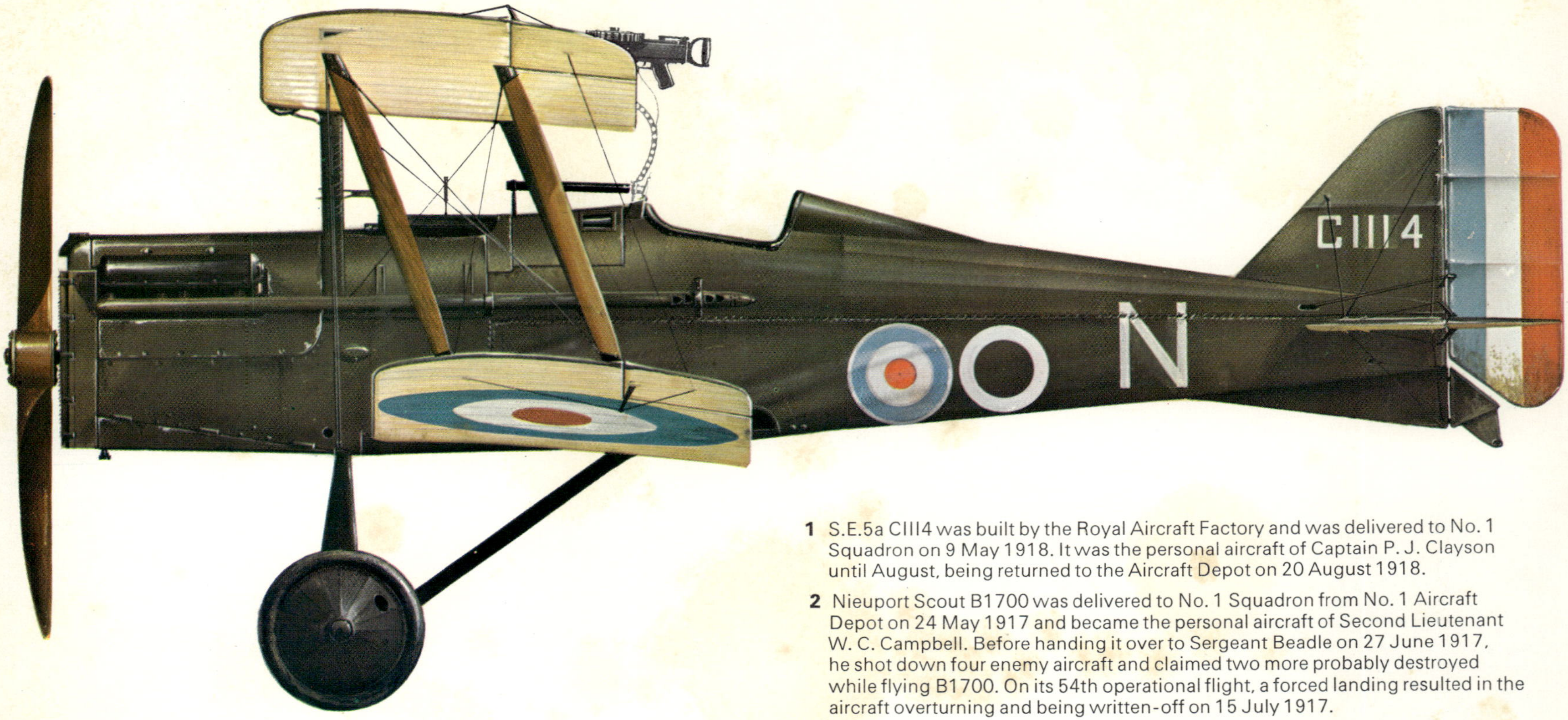

1 S.E.5a CIII4 was built by the Royal Aircraft Factory and was delivered to No. 1 Squadron on 9 May 1918. It was the personal aircraft of Captain P. J. Clayson until August, being returned to the Aircraft Depot on 20 August 1918.

2 Nieuport Scout B1700 was delivered to No. 1 Squadron from No. 1 Aircraft Depot on 24 May 1917 and became the personal aircraft of Second Lieutenant W. C. Campbell. Before handing it over to Sergeant Beadle on 27 June 1917, he shot down four enemy aircraft and claimed two more probably destroyed while flying B1700. On its 54th operational flight, a forced landing resulted in the aircraft overturning and being written-off on 15 July 1917.

3 Hawker Hurricane IIC BE215 was the personal aircraft of Squadron Leader J. A. F. MachLachlan between October 1941 and May 1942. It carried his personal insignia and flew its last intruder mission on 1 May 1942, being damaged on the following day and not repaired.

2

3

1

1 Hawker Siddeley Harrier XV788 carries revised matt camouflage with the white deleted from roundels and flashes to reduce the risk of Harriers being sighted on their dispersal sites. XV788 bears the legend 'Flt Lt M. P. Shaw' on its port side below the cockpit.

2 Hawker Fury K2047 was one of the initial batch of Furies (K2035 to K2051) delivered to No. 1 Squadron in February 1932. It crashed after a collision near Northolt on 23 April 1934.

3 Hawker Typhoon IB EJ974 spent a month with No. 1 Squadron before being passed on to No. 3 Tactical Exercise Unit on 24 April 1944.

2

3

to assist the French anti-aircraft gunners to recognize Hurricanes. In the evening the squadron flew to Cherbourg for two days to patrol the approaches of the port and protect the ships arriving with men and material for the B.E.F. At the end of September a move was made to Norrent-Fontes near St. Omer where the R.F.C. had flown twenty years earlier. But, within a few days No. 1 was transferred to Vassincourt, near Bar-le-Duc. No. 73 Squadron occupied Rouvres, 15 miles east of Verdun and No. 1 used this airfield as an advanced base for patrols. On 15 October, Squadron Leader 'Bull' Halahan led a patrol for 40 miles into Germany without meeting anything but anti-aircraft artillery *flak*. However, the last day of October brought the squadron's first success in the Second World War.

Three enemy aircraft had been sighted at high altitude when a section of Hurricanes was scrambled to intercept. Pilot Officer 'Boy' Mould managed to overtake one at 18,000 feet over Toul and surprised it. After a long burst the Dornier Do 17 caught fire and dived into the ground.

Patrols were routine until 23 November when enemy aircraft began to be plotted. Squadron Leader Halahan flying L1905 and Flying Officer Brown in L1971 intercepted a Do 17 near Metz and closed for attack. The German reconnaissance-bomber caught fire and crashed near St. Avold in the Maginot Line. Flying Officer Palmer in L1925 attacked another Dornier near Chalons and two of the crew baled out. Palmer flew alongside the weaving Dornier, its pilot lolling in his seat, to check details of armament and markings. Suddenly the enemy aircraft throttled back and Palmer overshot. The German pilot left his seat and put a burst of fire from the observer's front gun into the Hurricane. With a dead engine, Palmer force-landed near St. Ménehould. Two more Hurricanes attacked and the Dornier belly-landed near Palmer's Hurricane with over 500 bullet holes in it; *Unteroffizier* Arno Frankenberger stepped out into the arms of the French army. The squadron rescued him from the local jail and took him to the Officer's Mess for dinner in recognition of a very brave effort.

The third enemy brought down was a Heinkel He 111 sighted by a section of 'B' Flight and overtaken on the frontier. As it went down smoking, six French Morane-Saulnier M.S.406s dived into the fray, knocking off the starboard elevator and half the rudder of L1842 to the consternation of Sergeant Clowes. He had to land at 120 m.p.h. and tipped up at the end of his run. The He 111 crashed near Boulay but as both No. 73 Squadron and the Moranes claimed to have fired at it, the credit was apportioned three ways.

Throughout the hard winter patrols were kept up and March was signalled by increased enemy activity. On 2 March, Red Section sighted a Dornier near Nancy. Flying Officer Hilly Brown in L1974 was preparing to engage when smoke gushed out from his engine and the r.p.m. increased. He throttled back and glided to Nancy where he belly-landed. Inspection of the propeller proved it was no longer there, the two-blade unit having apparently worked loose.

Pilot Officer Mitchell in L1671 attacked the Dornier but his engine also started smoking. The third member of the section, Sergeant Soper in L1843, expended all his ammunition and then caught up with Mitchell, directing him by radio to a suitable landing ground. Unfortunately Mitchell lowered his wheels instead of belly-landing and was killed in the crash-landing near Sarre Union. The Dornier came down at La Petite Pierre but both Hurricanes were written-off. Next day, an He 111 was shot down near Forbach and blown up by its crew.

By the end of the second week in March all the squadron's aircraft had rear armour plate installed. It did nothing for the performance but increased the pilots' confidence considerably. At the end of the month the squadron met the Messerschmitt Bf 109s for the first time when Flying Officers Palmer, Richey (flying N2380 and N2382 respectively) and Pilot Officer Matthews (N2326) found two Bf 109s at 25,000 feet over Metz. From 1,000 feet above, the enemy turned to attack. As Palmer banked steeply to engage them, he spun and lost 12,000 feet before recovering and climbing back. Paul Richey managed to get astern of one Messerschmitt and saw it begin to smoke and go down in a vertical spiral. Another Bf 109 arrived and prevented the crash of the first being seen.

The same afternoon. Flight Lieutenant Walker (N2382, again in action), Flying Officer Stratton (N2334) and Sergeant Clowes (L1969) sighted aircraft near Metz which turned out to be Messerchmitt Bf 110 *Zerstörer* (Destroyer) two-motor fighters in three sections of three. The three Hurricanes attacked and Walker hit one Bf 110 and observed an engine beginning to smoke. Stratton fired at the same escort-fighter and the other engine caught fire. By now the wildly weaving Messerschmitts were down to 2,000 feet and the Hurricanes were out of ammunition so that the dog-

1 The Commanding Officer's Fury carried no identification letter but had a squadron leader's pennant on the fin. (*Photo: Flight International 12928.*)

2 No. 1 Squadron's aerobatic team Furies were in standard colour schemes in contrast to more modern trends. (*Photo: Ministry of Defence H.1144.*)

1

2

fight ended. A Messerschmitt pilot was picked up by the French after parachuting. Throughout the engagement no fire was seen from the rear gunners and they seemed to have been immobilised by the effects of 'g' (gravitational force) during the hectic manoeuvres of the battle.

As April opened, more fighters were encountered. A section consisting of Flight Lieutenant Hanks, Clisby and Mould encountered nine Bf 110s and saw three go down to their eight gun armament. However, none was found on Allied territory. Next day six Hurricanes were chasing two enemy aircraft near St. Avold when they were 'jumped' by Bf 109s. Flying Officer Palmer (in N2326 previously noted) was hit in his reserve tank and the Hurricane caught fire. The pilot baled out and arrived safely 500 yards on the right side of the front line. Clisby in L1927 fired at the enemy fighter responsible and saw it dive vertically into cloud with smoke pouring out. Kilmartin in L1685 saw the fighter he attacked go down through cloud and crash in Puttelange. This was later reported to be Palmer's abandoned Hurricane and the fate of the Messerschmitt was unknown.

On 10 May, the German offensive opened, The squadron was in the air all day and every flyable aircraft, even though unarmed, took off to avoid being attacked on the ground as waves of German bombers passed overhead. Four enemy bombers were shot down but two Hurricanes had to force-land and another was abandoned when the pilot baled-out. At mid-day, No. 1 was ordered to move back to Berry-au-Bac airfield near Reims where it was less exposed.

Next day, 'B' Flight caught a formation of Bf 110s and destroyed three while, later in the day 'A' Flight engaged 15 Bf 110s escorting a bomber formation near Mezieres. After the ensuing dogfight, the wreckages of 10 Messerschmitts and Paul Richey's Hurricane were found in the area—the latter having been set on fire by five Bf 110s. The pilot parachuted safely.

The primary purpose of the A.A.S.F. fighter squadrons was to provide cover for the bomber formations but in the confused situation this was seldom practicable. When, on 14 May, 'A' Flight went out to protect Battles and Blenheims attacking the bridges at Sedan, they were fully occupied in defending themselves against formations of enemy fighters. Thirteen enemy aircraft were claimed during the day but two pilots were missing and another Hurricane had crash-landed. On 15/16 May, Berry-au-Bac was heavily bombed and on 17 May it was evacuated. The squadron's Hurricanes headed for Condé-Vraux, south of Reims, and joined No. 114 Squadron's three surviving Blenheims. The ground crews set off for Anglure further south, burning two abandoned Hurricanes before leaving. Two days later, on 19 May, they were joined by the aircraft.

After 10 days of action, most of the original pilots who had survived were replaced by others freshly posted from the U.K. In those 10 days, two pilots had been killed, two wounded and one captured. Claims for enemy aircraft totalled 114 for the same period. On 24 May, the mainstay of the squadron left; Halahan, Hanks, Walker, Kilmartin, Stratton, Palmer and Mould. Their replacements were keen but combat inexperienced and when Flight Lieutenant Warcup led eleven newly-arrived pilots over Arras to look for dive-bombers they ran into heavy *flak* at 2,000 feet. He ordered the squadron to open formation but flew into cloud and emerged to find six Bf 109s. About the same moment he also made the unhappy discovery that the squadron he was leading was no longer behind him and had to make a hurried retreat. The other 11 fighter pilots, having 'lost' their leader, and finding no dive-bombers, completed their flying time and returned to base. Squadron Leader D. A. Pemberton took over as C.O. with three replacement and 12 new pilots but the period was hardly propitious for training what was virtually a new squadron. Up to this date, 38 aircraft had been written-off by the squadron—though all but 10 could have been repaired had conditions permitted speedy removal to a maintenance unit.

Early in June the fighters were withdrawn to Chateaudun and airfields in the Rouen area were used only as refuelling bases for squadrons covering the troops standing on the Somme line. When this line broke, the ground personnel moved back to Nantes for evacuation while the remaining R.A.F. fighters tried to keep the air clear over St. Nazaire and Brest. On 16 June, about 250 men of No. 1 Squadron left Brest for Plymouth and the remainder were evacuated through La Rochelle next day. At 11.45 on 18 June, the last of No. 1's Hurricanes left St. Nazaire and flew to Tangmere. The ground staff travelled to Northolt where they were joined by the squadron pilots and for the rest of the month No. 1 refitted in preparation for the uncertain future.

From Defence to Offence

On the first day of July 1940, No. 1 Squadron began to fly operational patrols from Northolt. The opening stages of the German attack on Britain consisted of attacks on convoys in the English Channel and coastal towns. Operating from Northolt, the squadron had few chances to intercept enemy aircraft until it moved to Tangmere to replace No. 43 Squadron on 23 July. Two days later, Flight Lieutenant H. B. L. Hillcoat (in P3044) was leading a section consisting also of Flying Officer H. N. E. Salmon (P3684) and Pilot Officer G. E. Goodman (P2686). Off the Dorset coast the Hurricanes ran into Bf 109s escorting a raid on Portland. In the ensuing engagement, Hillcoat expended all his ammunition without apparent result. Salmon fired half his bullets at a Bf 109 which spun away. At 2,000 feet, the British pilot blacked out and the Messerschmitt was not seen again. Goodman was attacked by a Bf 109 which stalled while manoeuvring near the sea and dived into the water with the loss of *Oberleutnant* Kirstein of III./J.G.27.

On 1 August, bases were exchanged with No. 43 Squadron and No. 1 returned to Northolt but began to use forward airfields at Tangmere, Hawkinge and Manston (Kent) for patrols. Three sections were patrolling south of Tangmere on 11 August when they were attacked from above by enemy fighters. The squadron broke formation and Pilot Officers Goodman and Chetham (flying P2686 and P2548) found a Bf 110D of *Zerstörergeschwader 2* (*Z.G.2*—Destroyer *Geschwader 2*) and attacked from astern. From the rear cockpit came a strange apparatus which appeared to be a drogue trailing about 2000 yards of wire. It missed both Hurricanes and the Messerschmitt caught fire, hitting the water. The result was photographed by Goodman but curiously the loss was not recorded by the Germans, only two Bf 110s being shown as damaged. One of these was presumably that attacked by Flight Lieutenant M. H. Brown in P3047. Half an hour later, Pilot Officer J. A. J. Davey's Hurricane P3172 attempted to force-land near Sandown, Isle of Wight, after being attacked by Bf 109s but crashed, killing the pilot.

On 15 August, the *Luftwaffe* launched its biggest attack of the battle. No. 1 Squadron moved forward to North Weald and was 'scrambled' to intercept a raid approaching Harwich. This consisted of 16 Bf 110s and nine Bf 109 fighter-bombers belonging to *Erprobungsgruppe 210* (Experimental *Gruppe*) heading for Martlesham Heath airfield near Woodbridge, Suffolk. Unfortunately the nine Hurricanes arrived too late and were 'jumped' by the Bf 109s which had dropped their bombs and were on their way home. Three Hurricanes went down into the sea and only Flight Lieutenant Mark Brown was picked up. The enemy escaped apparently without loss though three fighters claimed damage to enemy aircraft.

The squadron's luck was still not in evidence next day when it was 'scrambled' to intercept a raid approaching over the Isle of Wight. A skirmish with Bf 109s over Selsey Bill was indecisive and Pilot Officer J. F. Elkington's Hurricane P3173 was hit by anti-aircraft fire, the pilot baling out over Thorney Island. As this was going on, a formation of Junkers Ju 87 dive-bombers wrecked Tangmere though they lost seven of their number in the process.

In the late afternoon, He 111s crossed the coast near Brighton (Sussex) and were sighted by a patrol. Squadron Leader Pemberton (in P2751), leading 12 Hurricanes in a head-on attack, set fire to an He 111P with his first burst. His own Merlin engine caught fire but the flames died before he could bale out and a successful landing was made. Pilot Officer Goodman (in P2686) saw an He 111 crash near Petworth and, ironically, while circling the wreck at 500 feet his own Hurricane was damaged as the enemy bomber exploded. Flying Officer Salmon (in P3678) attacked a Bf 110 which immediately went into a vertical dive. In turn, when refuelling at Redhill (Surrey), his Hurricane was bombed by a Do 17 but without being damaged. Pilot Officer C. M. Stavert (flying P3782) reported encountering an He 111 head-on in cloud. He fired and the bomber dived steeply away. On breaking cloud, burning wreckage was seen below. Claims for four He 111s and a Junkers Ju 88 were lodged. One He 111 was confirmed while two Bf 110s and a second He 111 were recorded lost by the Germans in unknown circumstances and may have been among the squadron's claims.

On the afternoon of 18 August, the squadron was ordered to North Weald (Essex). Over Southend No. 1 Squadron met a dozen Bf 109s of J.G.51 and Squadron Leader Pemberton chased one at low level across Kent, finally seeing it crash near Tenterden (Kent). Later a raid was reported near Shoreham (Sussex) and about 60 Do 17s were intercepted over the South Downs. Blue Section set upon a Do 17 whose crew baled-out. Goodman saw a Bf 110 heading south with its port engine trailing smoke. He attacked and set the starboard engine on fire, after which the enemy fighter crashed into the sea.

German bombers were raiding by night and as the Blenheim night fighters were lacking in performance Hurricanes and Spitfires had been making night flights. The effectiveness of the London balloon barrage was unfortunately demonstrated on the night of 19 August when Pilot Officer C. N. Birch (P3684) hit a cable and he had to bale out. Landing on a rooftop in north London's Finchley, he was rescued by the fire brigade.

Intercepting bombers at night was no easy matter and, once found, they could be easily lost in the darkness. Sergeant H. J. Merchant pursued three enemy bombers on the night of 22/23 August unsuccessfully, eventually having to force-land and P2980 near Maidstone (Kent) by the aid of parachute flares after running out of fuel.

One of No.1 Squadron's last battles in the south occurred on 6 September when Flight Lieutenant Mark Brown (in veteran L1934) was leading a patrol of nine Hurricanes near Kenley. A group of Ju 88s escorted by Bf 110s had attacked the Hawker factory aerodrome at Brooklands without doing much damage and were returning home when sighted. Pilot Officers R. H. Dibnah and G. E. Goodman each destroyed a Bf 110 of *Z.G. 26* but, in turn, Goodman was surprised by enemy fighters and had to bale out.

Three days later, 15 Hurricanes left Northolt on detachment to Wittering (Northamptonshire) and were joined on September 20 by the rest of the squadron. Two months of intensive flying in the front line of Britain's defence had made a rest period overdue and in the following weeks few enemy aircraft were seen. Pilot Officer A. V. Clowes was one pilot who got a glimpse of the enemy when he met a Ju 88 emerging from a cloud near Hendon. The enemy bomber turned and 'fled'; which was fortunate since Clowes was flying the squadron's 'hack'—a Miles Magister elementary trainer—at the time.

No. 1's flying roster in October would have caused many raised eyebrows a year before. A large proportion of the pilots were Poles and Czechoslovaks. One exception to the rule was Lieutenant Jean Demozay who rejoined No. 1 Squadron on 16 October. During the squadron's stay in France, Demozay had joined it as an interpreter and liaison officer with the *Armée de l'Air*. A few days before France accepted an armistice, he discovered a barely-flyable two-motor Bristol Bombay transport and brought 15 British soldiers back to England. Having been a civil transport pilot before the war he passed rapidly through the R.A.F. training system and became a fighter pilot. Using a cover name of 'Moses Morlaix' to protect relatives in France from possible German reprisals, he came back to his old squadron and on 8 November caught a Ju 88 over The Wash and set one engine on fire. By the time he was posted to North Africa to train pilots for the Free French Air Force in February 1943, he was a Wing Commander and credited with 21 enemy aircraft destroyed.

On 15 December, the squadron returned to Northolt but moved a few weeks later to Kenley. 9 January 1941, marked No. 1's first offensive 'sweep' over Northern France when nine of its Hurricanes joined 12 of 615 Squadron for a tour up the French coast from Cap Gris Nez to Calais without reaction from the *Luftwaffe*. Small forces of bombers began to be escorted and conversion to improved Hurricane IIAs started to take place in February. These sweeps were occasionally relieved by 'Rhubarbs', a code-name which applied to a small number of aircraft attacking 'targets of opportunity'. On one such operation, Wing Commander J. R. A. Peel (in Z2525) led six Hurricanes over the Le Touquet area. Three became separated in cloud and emerged over Berck airfield where three Bf 109s were machine-gunned.

A name which was to reappear frequently in No. 1 Squadron's records was that of Sergeant Karel Kuttelwascher. On 8 April, four Hurricanes patrolling over Dungeness sighted enemy fighters across the Channel and intercepted them. Flying Z2464, 'Kut', as he became known throughout Fighter Command, sprayed two short bursts into a yellow-nosed Bf 109 which dived into a small wood 15 miles south of Cap Gris Nez.

Night flying continued and on the night of 10/11 May, large number of enemy bombers over the London area presented No. 1 with several targets. Twelve Hurricanes were operating in three sections of four each from Redhill. Squadron Leader R. E. P. Brooker (in Z2625) spotted an He 111 coming up the Thames Estuary, an excellent aerial signpost to London. Closing from 200 yards to point-blank range and firing into the bomber, he saw the port engine catch fire. Further attacks were prevented by oil from the stricken Heinkel covering the Hurricane's windscreen.

Moses Demozay was flying Z2909 in the same area when another He 111 was coned by searchlights over London's East India Docks. Closing in to 30 yards astern, he set fire to the port engine and the enemy bomber dived into the ground on the south bank of the Thames. Sergeant Dygryn took Z2687 into a beam attack on an He 111 three times and the Heinkel crashed near Kenley. Three other pilots fired at enemy bombers while eight more Hurricanes patrolling over their base were also in action.

Sergeant Dygrin spent 40 minutes refuelling and rearming and was off again to find another He 111 heading south over Kenley. After an attack from dead astern, it burst into flames and spun into the ground. Pilot Officer Raymond, a New Zealander flying Z2482, was looking below when his Hurricane rocked and tracer bullets began flashing past. A He 111 was above him at which he fired before it disappeared in a steep dive.

Flight Lieutenant Jackman (in Z3241) chased a London-bound He 111 for three miles before getting close enough to fire. The bomber turned south but after the third burst dived into the ground about 15 miles south of Redhill. At 03:15, Dygryn was off for the third time and found a Ju 88 north-east of Biggin Hill. Attacked at point-blank range, the bomber began to smoke and over the coast burst into flames and dived into the sea about 10 miles south of Hastings. The gallant pilot was awarded the Czech War Cross and Medal for Gallantry by Dr. Benes, the President of Czechoslovakia (and in March 1942 the Distinguished Flying Medal) but was reported missing on 4 June 1942

1 Pilots of No. 1 Squadron at Wittering; from left to right Pilot Officers Coats, Davies, Greenhalgh, Dixon, Flight Lieutenant McEvoy, Pilot Officer Peck, not known, Pilot Officers Wurtele and Rabagliati. Note the squadron badge carried on the fin of K2048. (*Photo: Wittering No. A09994.*)

2 Hurricane IICs in formation about May 1942 carry small serials and darkened camouflage for intruder duties. (*Photo: Aeroplane.*)

3 Hurricane IIC Z3897 with normal-size serial served with No. 1 Squadron between July 1941 and June 1942. (*Photo: Ministry of Supply E(MoS) 491.*)

4 Hurricane I P3395 in its dispersal pen at Wittering in October 1940. Flying Officer A. V. Clowes, DFM, (in cockpit) used a wasp as his personal insignia, each enemy aircraft destroyed resulting in an extra stripe on its body. (*Photo: I.W.M. 17331.*)

1 Shortly before re-equipment with Meteor F.8s took place, squadron badges were permitted to reappear on aircraft. On Meteor F.4 VT178, the badge, flanked by small bars, decorated the nose. (*Photo: No. 1 Squadron archives.*)

2 Another '1' formation, this time with Meteor F.8s along the Sussex coast. (*Photo: Flight International 26743.*)

3 Meteor F.4s at Tangmere in 1949 still carry the squadron's wartime code letters 'JX'. (*Photo: Flight International 22352.*)

4 No. 1 Squadron re-enact their 1918-style squadron photograph with Spitfire F.21s at Wittering in 1946. Note small serials carried above the fin flashes. (*Photo: No. 1 Squadron archives.*)

3

1

4

2

while on an intruder mission to Evreux.

In July, the squadron returned to its home airfield at Tangmere where it began the frustrating task of training with Douglas Havocs fitted with airborne searchlights. The idea was that the Havoc would locate an enemy bomber by radar and illuminate it for the Hurricane to shoot down. The theory did not work out in practice and had no success though a large number of flying hours was spent in training.

Despite its preoccupation with night fighting, February 1942, found the squadron impressed into a completely different role. The German battle-cruisers *KM Scharnhorst* and *KM Gneisenau*, accompanied by the heavy cruiser *KM Prinz Eugen*, left Brest early on 12 February to run the gauntlet of the English Channel to reach German ports. The alternative was to put out into the Atlantic and spend days on a hazardous voyage round the north of Scotland. Nobody on the German naval staff had any illusions as to the dangers involved—the fate of the *Bismarck* being too fresh in their memories. It was decided to pass through the Strait of Dover in daylight under strong fighter escort. Full of foreboding the ships' captains prepared for a passage through seas dominated by British sea and air power.

In the event, nothing happened to disturb the German force until it had passed the worst section. The submarines and patrol aircraft—dogged by unserviceability and withdrawal of units for other tasks—failed to locate the enemy ships. Only a pair of Spitfires of R.A.F. Fighter Command on a coastal sweep sighted the ships and by then they were off Le Touquet. A hastily-assembled striking force of bombers from Bomber Command, torpedo-bombers from the Fleet Air Arm, old destroyers and light coastal craft was unable to make any impression. Most of the aircraft lost their escort in the murk and many failed to find their targets. No. 1 Squadron despatched six aircraft of 'A' Flight at short notice led by Flight Lieutenant W. Raymond and covered by 12 Spitfires of 129 Squadron. They attacked three destroyers of the screen in the face of intense *flak* and lost two of their number, one of the pilots being picked up and taken prisoner. Apart from 20-mm cannon fire, they had no means of damaging enemy ships and the lack of co-ordination between the various forces summoned up to attack meant that the squadron's effort made little if any difference to the outcome. All three ships reached port but *KM Gneisenau* hit a mine and never sailed again.

'Kut', now a Flight Lieutenant, opened a remarkable series of intruder raids over French airfields on 1 April when he took off in his Hurricane II (BE581) from Tangmere and flew to Evreux. Seeing no activity, he sent on to Melun/Villaroche, south of Paris, where the flarepath was illuminated. Two minutes after he arrived, a Ju 88 took off and closing to 100 yards Kuttelwascher fired. Its starboard engine exploded and the bomber dived into the ground. By the end of the month, he had accounted for three more and two probably destroyed by using the same tactics.

Squadron Leader J. A. F. MacLachlan, DFC and Bar, was another highly successful intruder pilot. He used to fly his Hurricane (BE215) on these dangerous night missions despite an artificial left arm, the result of being shot down over Malta in February 1941. While with No. 1 Squadron, he destroyed five enemy bombers near their airfields. 'Kut' advanced his own tally to 13 night victories, this excluding three fighters during earlier daylight operations.

During July 1942, the Hurricanes flew their last intruder missions and the squadron moved to Acklington in Northumberland, there to convert to Hawker Typhoons. Powered by the new Napier Sabre 24-cylinder engine of over 2,000 horse-power, Hawker's new fighter was the fastest fighter yet delivered to the R.A.F., with a top speed of over 400 m.p.h. It was received by the squadron with mixed feelings. Whereas its speed enabled it to intercept enemy fighter-bombers at low altitude—making fleeting raids on English coastal targets—the exigencies of war had resulted in the type being pressed into service before full development had been carried out. Nos. 56 and 609 Squadrons at Duxford had experienced serious problems with both the new aero-engine and the airframe. Engine failures were common. Also noxious gases from the engine had affected pilots, sometimes ending in an aircraft diving into the ground with the pilot unconscious. The rear fuselage was found to be weak and several Typhoons lost their tails until modifications had strengthened this area.

Many of the drawbacks had been overcome before No. 1 took delivery of Typhoons and its speed and fire-power were evident when the first enemy aircraft were encountered on 9 September. A pair of Typhoons on patrol off the Yorkshire coast were vectored on to two Messerschmitt Me 210 fighter-bombers—the Luftwaffe equivalent of the de Havilland Mosquito. Despite their own turn of speed, both Me 210s were successfully intercepted and shot down off the coast.

In February 1943, the squadron moved south to use the Typhoon's speed as a counter to Focke-Wulf FW 190s attacking towns on the south coast. Standing patrols were flown by pairs of Typhoons as the few minutes during which such 'hit-and-run' attacks took place did not permit fighters to be scrambled from their airfields with any chance of successful interception.

The Typhoon's reputation was to be made in quite a different role. Armed with underwing rocket projectiles or bombs, the Typhoon squadrons began attacking German positions and transport in Northern France. A variety of targets bore the brunt of the assault—gun positions, trains, road convoys, headquarters, radar stations, coastal shipping, and, from the beginning of 1944, strange structures appearing in the Pas-de-Calais on the French side of the Dover Strait. These were the launching sites for the notorious 'V-1's'.

The efforts of the Typhoon squadrons reached their peak in the days after the Allied landings in Normandy in June 1944 but by that time No. 1 Squadron had changed its Typhoons for Supermarine Spitfires. In April 1944, it had converted to Spitfire IX fighter-bombers equipped with racks for 500-lb bombs. Based in the South-West, it operated over Brittany until June.

On 24 June, two days after it had hurriedly moved to Detling (Kent) No. 1 put up its first 'anti-Diver' patrol. 'Diver' was the code-name allocated to the new 'V-1' flying-bomb whose arrival had been predicted by intelligence sources and air reconnaissance. The 'Revenge Weapon' launching ramps and stores areas had been pounded by bombers for six months and many were inoperative. But sufficient sites remained to despatch the first wave. The Argus pulse-jet, mounted on top of the cigar-shaped fuselage crammed with fuel and high-explosive, heralded its pilotless approach with a characteristic throbbing note that seemed to add to its inhuman aspect.

Three days later, a trio of the squadron's Spitfires shot down No. 1's first flying-bomb near Wadhurst. Its speed was high enough to make it difficult to intercept and overtake; its size required accurate shooting and its load of explosives could be lethal if it blew up while an attacking fighter was too close. There were other hazards, ranging from collision with other fighters intent on their targets, invisible cables on the barrage balloons and anti-aircraft fire which opened up while fighters were still pursuing their quarry.

Flight Sergeant I. Hastings was flying MK997 near Beachy Head on 5 July when he spotted a flying-bomb coming in over Beachy Head. He pursued it as far as Gatwick where he succeeded in blowing off the V-1's port wing so that it dived into the ground. As the Spitfire broke away it hit the cable of one of the balloons of the barrage guarding the approaches to London and spun round it. Fortunately, the pilot was able to right the aircraft and returned to base with an amputated wing-tip.

The combination of fighter areas, gun and balloon belts eventually succeeded in destroying a large proportion of the incoming V-1s and in September the launching sites were overrun by the British and Canadian armies as they broke out of Normandy and drove the German army back to the German frontier. The squadron's Spitfires were equipped with long-range tanks and escorted Bomber Command's Avro Lancasters and Handley Page Halifaxes on their daylight raids over Germany for the rest of the war, often using captured airfields in Belgium to permit deeper penetrations into the dwindling territory of the *Third Reich*. By the end of April 1945, targets had become scarce and operational flying drew to a close.

Within a few days of the German surrender, No. 1 was the recipient of new Spitfire 21s, one of the last variants of the superb line of Spitfires with twice the horse-power of the Mark I and a top speed of over 450 m.p.h. These No. 1 took home to Tangmere in April 1946 to find the airfield much changed from that day in September 1939 when the squadron flew off to war. Concrete runways scarred the green grass, the old hangars had been flattened by *Stuka* dive-bombers and No. 43 Squadron was in some improbable location in Southern Austria. That things had changed was made abundantly clear just over a year later.

In October 1946, No. 1 Squadron abandoned piston-engined aircraft and began flying jet-propelled Gloster Meteor fighters. Powered by two Rolls-Royce Derwent Is, the top speed was only 25 m.p.h. faster than the Spitfire 21 but the next mark had set up a World Speed Record of over 600 m.p.h. and armed operational Mark 4s could reach 590 m.p.h.

In August 1947, the squadron converted once more. But not, to their dismay, to faster Meteors. By what could only be a grotesque lack of historical knowledge, apparent to every member of the squadron, No. 1 (Fighter) Squadron had been selected as No. 11 Group's instrument training unit. The enormity of the crime became even more evident when it was learned that the aircraft to be used for this purpose were sedate North American Harvard and Airspeed Oxford trainers.

It was nearly two years before the Air Ministry relented and gave the squadron back its fighters—in the shape of sleek silver Meteor F.4s. In February 1949, No. 43 Squadron reappeared and Tangmere's private and exclusive war between the two old rivals was resumed. Finally, in 1950, squadron markings were allowed to adorn the Meteors and fighter squadrons blossomed out in a variety of colourful emblems.

The serious side of the squadron's activities kept it busy exercising its aircraft as part of the air defences. The shadow of the nuclear bomb hung over defence planning. No longer could a heavy toll be taken of successive enemy attacks to bring an air offensive to a halt. Where A-bombs were part of the hostile intruder's armoury, 100% was the minimum loss that could be inflicted on the enemy for fighter defence to be effective. With the equipment available and the short warning provided, it could never be so.

By the end of 1955, Hawker Hunter swept-wing fighters had replaced the ageing Meteors. No. 1's version was Hunter F.5 with an Armstrong-Siddeley Sapphire engine—the majority of Hunters being powered by the Rolls-Royce Avon. For nearly three years the Hunter F.5 served the squadron until, on 23 June 1958, No. 1 Squadron was disbanded.

Ground Attack

That the R.A.F. would be incomplete without a No. 1 Squadron was now recognized in all quarters, which was why the hapless No. 263 Squadron was informed that with effect from 23 June 1958 it was No. 1 Squadron. Such traumatic experiences had by now become frequent and the new No. 1 Squadron continued to fly its Hunter F.6s from Stradishall (Suffolk) without visible mental anguish.

In March 1960, signs of a change of role appeared in the shape of a Hunter FGA. 9. The airframe was a Mark 6 but provision was made for the carriage on underwing racks of bombs, rockets and long-range tanks. The role designated by the FGA prefix was fighter-ground attack and it was the modern equivalent of the wartime fighter-bombers.

A result of the advent of this specialised Hunter was the removal of No. 1 Squadron (along with No. 54 Squadron) from Fighter Command to the incongruous surroundings of R.A.F. Transport Command. To cater for close-support of the army, No. 38 Group, Transport Command had a variety of types. These included: Westland Whirlwind and Wessex helicopters for lifting troops and supplies into the battle area; Bristol Belvedere heavy-lift helicopters; and, Scottish Aviation Pioneer and Twin Pioneer short take-off and landing (STOL) transports and liaison types. A ground-attack arm was required and two Hunter squadrons were allotted to this task, namely Nos. 1 and 54 Squadrons.

By June 1960, conversion to FGA.9s was complete and the squadron began intensive training exercises in support of the army which necessitated frequent moves around the U.K. and to the European continent to test and improve upon the mobility that was essential for the army support role. Transport Command became Air Support Command, a more appropriate title for its responsibilities, and cheated those who had hoped one day to be able to spread incredulity on some foreign airfield by appearing in single-seat fighters emblazoned with the words 'R.A.F. Transport Command'.

Close-support for army units means operating from as far forward as possible to reduce the reaction time to calls for aid. The need for runways tended to restrict ground-attack squadrons in this respect and it was left to No. 1 Squadron to make history by being the first fighter squadron to dispense with airfields completely.

The means to this end were provided by the brilliantly-conceived Hawker P.1127 which led to the Kestrel—and began flying tests on 21 October 1960—and was developed into the unique Harrier GR.1. Using a Bristol Siddeley Pegasus engine which could provide both forward thrust and vertical lift by means of swivelling ducts, a swept-wing ground-attack fighter could be operated from small clearings only a short distance behind the battle area. This cut reaction time to a minimum while conserving aircraft hours, the alternative being to keep standing patrols in the air awaiting a call for support.

In July 1969, No. 1 moved to Wittering (Northants.) and began converting to Harriers. Since the two-seat Harrier T.2 had not yet come into service, conversion had to be carried out without the benefit of these. Teething troubles inseparable to the introduction of any new type had to be overcome. But as soon as the squadron had its full establishment of aircraft, tactical trials began. The mobility conferred by the Harrier's ability to operate away from airfields meant that ground crews had to be able to maintain and re-arm aircraft without base facilities. Supply arrangements were developed with the helicopters and transport support units of No. 38 Group.

In March 1970, 10 Harriers left on their first overseas detachment. Staging through Istres (in Southern France), Malta and Suda Bay, Crete, they arrived at Akrotiri on 4 March to spend two weeks in Cyprus. A second visit to Cyprus in July allowed the weapons system to be tested on the local ranges during a six-week period and the squadron returned to make its first appearance with Harriers at the biennial Farnborough Show of the Society of British Aerospace Companies. Historically, they were flying over the same ground that the squadron had used for its first flights in 1912.

After a trip to Norway, eight Harriers visited the Nato armament training base at Decimomannu, Sardinia, in February 1971. Then, in May, No. 1 flew some of its aircraft aboard *HMS Ark Royal* for carrier trials. This was the first occasion since the war that an R.A.F. fighter squadron had operated off a carrier deck and an indication of a future role when the Royal Navy finally gives up its fixed-wing aircraft.

No. 1 Squadron's motto *In omnibus princeps* (Foremost in Everything) proved prophetic when it became the first vertical take-off fighter squadron in the world. It is also a curious coincidence that the squadron's first aircraft was also a vertical take-off type—albeit of the lighter-than-air variety.

1

2

1 Hunter F.5s in traditional squadron photograph order June 1956. (*Photo: No. 1 Sqdn archives.*)

2 Harriers in their element; three aircraft of No. 1 Sqdn take off from restricted space of Rome's old Ciampino airfield, now surrounded by houses. (*Photo: Hawker Siddeley Aviation 701942.*)

3 A quartet of Hunter FGA.9s fly low over Kyrenia harbour; each carries four long range tanks. (*Photo: No. 1 Squadron archives.*)

4 An echelon of Harrier GR.1s in original colour scheme before application of matt finish and deletion of white in roundels and fin flash. Four aircraft carry squadron badge above fin flash. (*Photo: Hawker Siddeley Aviation 700802.*)

5 Rocket-armed Harriers on armament trials. (*Photo: M.O.D. TN6344/37.*)

3

4

5

SQUADRON BASES

Farnborough, Hampshire	13 May 1912 to 1 May 1914
Brooklands, Surrey	1 August 1914
Netheravon, Wiltshire	— November 1914
St. Omer, France	7 March 1915
Bailleul, France	29 March 1915
St. Marie Cappel, France	29 March 1918
Clairmarais South, France	13 April 1918
Fienvillers, France	5 August 1918
Senlis, France	6 October 1918
Bouvincourt, France	26 October 1918
Izel-Le Hameau, France	18 November 1919
London Colney, Hertfordshire	1 March 1919
Uxbridge, Middlesex	— October 1919 to 20 January 1920
Risalpur, Peshawar, India	21 January 1920
Bangalore, Mysore, India	11 May 1920
Hinaidi, Iraq	1 May 1921 to 1 November 1926
Tangmere, Sussex	1 February 1927
Northolt, Middlesex	7 August 1928
Tangmere, Sussex	17 August 1928
Le Havre/Octeville, France	9 September 1939
Norrent Fontes, France	29 September 1939
Vassincourt, France	9 October 1939
Berry-au-Bac, France	11 April 1940
Vassincourt, France	19 April 1940
Berry-au-Bac, France	10 May 1940
Condé-Vraux, France	17 May 1940
Anglure, France	18 May 1940
Chateaudun, France	3 June 1940
Nantes, France	14 June 1940
St. Nazaire, France	17 June 1940
Northolt, Middlesex	18 June 1940
Tangmere, Sussex	23 July 1940
Northolt, Middlesex	1 August 1940
Wittering, Northamptonshire	9 September 1940
Northolt, Middlesex	15 December 1940
Kenley, Surrey	5 January 1941
Croydon, Surrey	7 April 1941
Redhill, Surrey	1 May 1941
Kenley, Surrey	1 June 1941
Redhill, Surrey	14 June 1941
Tangmere, Sussex	1 July 1941
Acklington, Northumberland	8 July 1942
Biggin Hill, Kent	9 February 1943
Lympne, Kent	15 March 1943
Martlesham Heath, Suffolk	15 February 1944
North Weald, Essex	3 April 1944
Ayr, Ayrshire	22 April 1944
Predannack, Cornwall	29 April 1944
Harrowbeer, Devonshire	20 June 1944
Detling, Kent	22 June 1944
Lympne, Kent	11 July 1944
Detling, Kent	10 August 1944
Manston, Kent	18 December 1944
Coltishall, Norfolk	8 April 1945
Ludham, Norfolk	14 May 1945
Hutton Cranswick, Yorkshire	23 July 1945
Hawkinge, Kent	24 September 1945
Hutton Cranswick, Yorkshire	22 October 1945
Tangmere, Sussex	30 April 1946
Akrotiri, Cyprus	7 August 1956
Nicosia, Cyprus	1 September 1956
Tangmere, Sussex	24 December 1956 to 23 June 1958
Stradishall, Suffolk	23 June 1958
Waterbeach, Cambridgeshire	7 November 1961
West Raynham, Norfolk	13 August 1963
Wittering, Northamptonshire	18 July 1969

SQUADRON EQUIPMENT
Period of Use & Typical Serial and Code Letters

Type	Period of Use	Serial and Code Letters
Non-rigid airships	May 1912 to April 1914	—
Misc. training types (Avro 504, Farman S.7, S.11, Bristol Boxkite, Bleriot XI, Caudron G.III, etc.)	May 1914 to March 1915	—
Avro 504	March 1915 to September 1915	2859
B.E.8	March 1915 to June 1915	2130
Bristol Scout	April 1915 to October 1915	4672
Caudron G.III	March 1915 to September 1915	5038
Martinsyde S.1	June 1915 to July 1915	748
Morane Parasol	March 1915 to January 1917	5006
Nieuport 12, 14	July 1916 to January 1917	5171
Morane Biplane	January 1916 to January 1917	5160
Nieuport 17	March 1916 to August 1916	
	January 1917 to December 1917	A130
Nieuport 27	August 1917 to January 1918	B6818
S.E.5a	January 1918 to March 1919	C8846 (M)
Sopwith Snipe	January 1920 to November 1926	H4896
Nieuport Nighthawk	January 1920 to April 1921	HR8544
Armstrong Whitworth Siskin IIIA	February 1927 to February 1932	J8635
Hawker Fury I	February 1932 to November 1938	K2041
Gloster Gladiator I	February 1937 to March 1937	K6131
Hawker Hurricane I	October 1938 to February 1941	P3395 (JX-B)
Hawker Hurricane IIA	February 1941 to June 1941	Z2502
Hawker Hurricane IIB	April 1941 to January 1942	
	June 1942 to September 1942	Z3496
Hawker Hurricane IIC	July 1941 to September 1942	BN232 (JX-R)
Hawker Typhoon IB	July 1942 to April 1944	JP685 (JX-O)
Supermarine Spitfire IXB	April 1944 to May 1945	MK997 (JX-F)
Supermarine Spitfire F.21	May 1945 to October 1945	LA277 (JX-A)
Gloster Meteor F.III	October 1946 to August 1947	EE421 (JX-A)
North American Harvard T.2B	August 1947 to June 1948	FX411 (JX-K)
Airspeed Oxford T.2	August 1947 to June 1948	LX132 (JX-N)
Gloster Meteor F.4	June 1948 to September 1950	RA449 (JX-A)
Gloster Meteor F.8	September 1950 to October 1955	WA856 (P)
Hawker Hunter F.5	September 1955 to June 1958	WP147 (G)
Hawker Hunter F.6	June 1958 to June 1960	XE584 (W)
Hawker Hunter FGA.9	March 1960 to July 1969	XG157 (Y)
Hawker Siddeley Harrier GR.1	July 1969 to date	XV749 (K)

COMMANDING OFFICERS

Major E.M.Maitland	13 May 1912
Major C.A.H.Longcroft	1 May 1914
Major W.G.H.Salmond	28 January 1915
Major P.B.Joubert de la Ferte	19 August 1915
Major G.F.Pretyman DSO	24 November 1915
Major G.C.St.P.de Dombasle	24 December 1916
Major A.Barton Adams	20 June 1917
Major W.E.Young	3 August 1918
S/Ldr. J.B.Graham MC, AFC	18 March 1920
S/Ldr. G.G.A.Williams	10 November 1922
S/Ldr. E.O.Grenfell MC, DFC, AFC,	8 October 1923
S/Ldr. E.D.Atkinson DFC, AFC	25 May 1924
S/Ldr. C.N.Lowe	19 April 1926
S/Ldr. E.D.Atkinson DFC, AFC	11 April 1927
S/Ldr. E.O.Grenfell MC, DFC, AFC	19 March 1928
S/Ldr. C.B.S.Spackman	27 July 1931
S/Ldr. R.W.Chappell MC	21 November 1933
S/Ldr. C.W.Hill	1 October 1934
F/Lt. T.R.McEvoy	31 January 1936
S/Ldr. C.W.Hill	1 December 1936
S/Ldr. F.R.D.Swain AFC	12 April 1937
S/Ldr. I.A.Bertram	15 January 1938
S/Ldr. P.J.H.Halahan DFC	17 April 1939
S/Ldr. D.A.Pemberton DFC	24 May 1940
S/Ldr. M.H.Brown DFC	10 November 1940
S/Ldr. R.E.P. Brooker DFC	23 April 1941
S/Ldr. J.A.F.Maclachlan DSO, DFC	3 November 1941
S/Ldr. R.C.Wilkinson DFM	31 July 1942
S/Ldr. A.Zweigbergk	30 May 1943
S/Ldr. J.Checketts DSO, DFC	3 April 1944
S/Ldr. H.P.Lardner-Burke DFC	29 April 1944
S/Ldr. D.G.Cox	11 January 1945
S/Ldr. R.S.Nash	21 April 1945
S/Ldr. H.R.Allen DFC	9 January 1946
S/Ldr. C.H.Macfie DFC	26 October 1946
S/Ldr. T.R.Burne DSO, DFC	15 July 1947
Major R.Olds USAF*	4 February 1949
S/Ldr. T.R.Burne DSO, DFC	1 October 1949
Major D.F.Smith USAF*	10 January 1950
S/Ldr. J.L.W.Ellacombe DFC	18 August 1950
S/Ldr. R.B.Morison DFC	21 November 1952
S/Ldr. D.I.Smith	27 July 1953
S/Ldr. F.W.Lister DSO, DFC	1 December 1953
S/Ldr. R.S.Kingsford	8 August 1956
S/Ldr. L.de Garis AFC	5 July 1958
S/Ldr. J.J.Phipps	1 December 1958
S/Ldr. P.V.Pledger	1 January 1961
S/Ldr. F.L.Travers-Smith	1 January 1963
S/Ldr. D.C.G.Brook	28 December 1964
S/Ldr. G.Jones	1 November 1966
S/Ldr. L.A.B.Baker	20 September 1968
W/Cdr. J.A.Mansell	10 April 1969
S/Ldr. L.A.B.Baker	21 May 1969
W/Cdr. D.Allison	4 August 1969
W/Cdr. K.W.Hayr AFC	1 January 1970

* USAF—United States Air Force; On exchange tour of duty

No.23 Squadron

No. 23 Squadron lines its Gamecocks up at Kenley in 1927. The distinctive eagle has begun to appear on the fins and the squadron colours on fuselage sides and on the top wing. (*Photo: No. 23 Squadron archives.*)

Fort Grange, on the outskirts of Gosport, Hampshire, was one of a ring of forts built during the 19th century to defend the naval base of Portsmouth. To the Royal Navy it was tantamount to treason even to have considered building them since the presence of an enemy army meant that a seaborne invasion had taken place. That, the senior service averred, was impossible since the Navy would be there to sink the enemy on the high seas. Nevertheless, the Palmerston plan went ahead and surrounded Portsmouth with forts, large and small.

Naturally, none was used for the purpose for which it had been built. They did, however, become utilitarian—for stowing way various units which were better away from the mainstream of a naval dockyard. Thus, in September 1915, Fort Grange prepared to house a new formation, No. 23 Squadron, Royal Flying Corps.

The Commanding Officer of the new squadron was Captain L. A. Strange, an experienced pilot who had been in France with the first echelon of the R.F.C. He was one of the few fighter pilots of that era, having flown a Martinsyde Scout armed with a Lewis gun at a time when there were not many machine-gun armed single-seaters in service. Undeterred by a hair-raising experience when, while attempting to change the drum on his Lewis by standing up in the cockpit, his aircraft inverted itself and left him hanging in space, he arrived to form a fighter squadron which soon received the same type of aircraft. Since hanging by one's fingers from a Lewis gun magazine (a device intended for easy removal and not for supporting a fully-grown man) was not an act to be repeated lightly, it seems doubtful if the squadron's Martinsydes were allowed to be armed. In fact, No. 23 went to war in B.E.2c reconnaissance biplanes.

During 1915, enemy airships had been increasingly active over Britain. To defend the country against these intruders the R.F.C. could only supply a few inadequate aircraft to supplement the anti-aircraft guns which were also few and far between. Night flying was in its infancy. When Second Lieutenant R. Yates flew to Sutton's Farm on the eastern approaches to London, his B.E.2c was armed with 20-lb. bombs and explosive darts. He arrived on 8 October and was later joined by Second Lieutenant J. C. Slessor, a future Marshal of the Royal Air Force.

On the evening of 13 October 1915, five Zeppelins left Germany to raid London, four reaching the city. Because of the short range of the defending aircraft, they were held on the ground until a Zeppelin was in the vicinity; once airborne, there was no way of directing the pilot to his target. Zeppelin L.15 bombed along a line from the Strand to Limehouse, pursued by a mobile anti-aircraft gun, and headed east over Essex. Slessor took off during a break in the fog which covered the Essex airfields but was too late; the Zeppelin was illuminated by searchlights over Romford but the B.E. was too slow to catch it before the lights were left behind and the enemy disappeared from sight. Flares had been ignited at Sutton's Farm which were just visible through the fog and as Slessor approached the airfield a searchlight attempted to illuminate the landing area. The result was a dazzling sheet of fog and a broken undercarriage from the inevitable crash-landing.

Such extraneous activities did not continue for long as specialized home defence squadrons were being formed. The major part of the squadron trained around a nucleus supplied by No. 14 Squadron with a variety of types of aircraft and in January 1916 received the first of its F.E.2bs.

Designed at the Royal Aircraft Factory at Farnborough, the F.E.2b was a large two-seat biplane powered by a 120 h.p. Beardmore pusher engine. As No. 23 received the first of these, the squadron moved to France to open the type's fighting career. As a fighter, the F.E. configuration was already obsolete but lack of a suitable interrupter gear had brought pusher designs into favour. The gunner in the nose cockpit had a wide field of fire but from astern the bulky engine left an extensive blind spot. A maximum speed of about 90 m.p.h. was barely adequate for fighting purposes but despite this the F.E.s gave a good account of themselves against the nimble German single-seaters with their forward-firing synchronized machine-guns.

No. 23 moved to France on 16 March 1916, and

1

2

3

4

1 Photographs of No. 23 Sqdn's Dolphins are rare; E4717 has squadron's identification marking, a white disc, aft of roundel and individual aircraft letter 'M'. (*Photo: No. 23 Sqdn archives.*)

2 Gamecock J-8409 in May 1929 had no fin eagle; note contemporary style of dividing letter from digits of serial number by a hyphen used by Glosters and Bristol; other manufacturers used a period, some did not segregate at all. (*Photo: Flt. Int. 7205.*)

3 Pair of No. 23 Sqdn Gamecocks at Northolt during 1929 Sassoon Cup contest. (*Photo: Flt. Int. 7125.*)

4 A pilot boards his Bulldog IIA at Kenley in 1931. (*Photo: Flt. Int. 10453.*)

5 This view of No. 23 Sqdn Gamecock shows rigging detail, fuel tanks under top wing and ring-and-bead gunsight. (*Photo: M.O.D. H1138.*)

6 The first Fairey Long Range Monoplane (J9479) flown by Commanding Officer of No. 23 Sqdn on first non-stop flight from Britain to India, April 1929. (*Photo: No. 23 Sqdn archives.*)

7 Intruding on line of Bulldogs at Kenley, three Hart Fighters received for operational testing as two-seat fighters. (*Photo: Flt. Int. 10456.*)

joined 13th Wing at Le Hameau near Arras. Formations of 'Fees' were assigned to escort the almost defenceless R.F.C. reconnaissance biplanes which had been suffering at the hands of the Fokkers. On 23 March, the squadron lost its first aircraft when a lone Fokker dived on a formation over Queant. The 'Fee' crashed but the crew escaped, the pilot being wounded. One expedient adopted was to fly with the B.E.s astern of the F.E.s covering their tails but such static methods were completely alien to the way fighter tactics were developing.

An alternative to close escort was to put up offensive patrols of fighters to engage hostile aircraft whenever they were sighted. This freed fighters from the vicinity of slow reconnaissance biplanes which multiplied as preparations for the Battle of the Somme built up. The tactics paid off by giving the R.F.C. command of the air over the battlefield for a short but vital period. Then improved German fighters began to appear in ever-increasing numbers and the 'Fees' were even more outclassed.

By the end of 1916, the squadron was ready to replace 'Fees' with single-seat Spads and, by April 1917, the last of the pushers departed. So too did the squadron's gunners, men who had literally stood up to enemy fighters in a 'bath-tub' cockpit which reached only to knee level. A strap anchored the

5

6

7

gunner while he hung out of the nacelle in attempts to bring his Lewis to bear. In the event of a nose-over on landing, they had nothing except a thin layer of plywood and a nose-wheel to prevent them being crushed between the ground and the heavy engine. They were the first of a long line of air gunners who manned the guns of many generations of R.A.F. aircraft and still are to be found in the Avro Shackletons of Strike Command in the 1970s.

The first Spad S.VIIs arrived during February, 7 flying into Vert Galand on 24 February. The 'Fees' continued reconnaissance flights to the end and went on to become night bombers with other squadrons. In addition to offensive patrols, No. 23's Spads were engaged in ground strafing enemy troops and transport, such low-level flying leading to overheating of the Hispano engines. Extra cooling was provided by additional holes cut in the cowling and every pilot flew with a mallet to unjam his machine-gun.

At more elevated levels, the squadron's pilots found the Spad to be a strong and manoeuvrable aircraft and many enemy aircraft fell to their guns. The single Vickers machine-gun on the S.VII was replaced by two Vickers on the Spad S.XIII which reached No. 23 in December 1917. The 220 h.p. Hispano giving a top speed of 135 m.p.h. Unfortunately, this bigger engine—almost twice the power of the 'Fee's' Beardmore—also suffered from various ailments and was prone to failure.

Despite this engine drawback, several pilots soon became 'Spad experts' in shooting down enemy aircraft. One was Captain A. E. McKay, who flew Spad B3560 at the end of 1917 as his personal aircraft. On 19 November, he attacked a pair of enemy two-seaters near Moorslede, choosing a yellow and grey D.F.W. for a beam attack, afterwards turning on to its tail. After firing 40 rounds—at only 15 yards range—he saw the enemy dive steeply and followed, only to be attacked from behind by the second German. The Spad made a climbing turn to get astern of the enemy which dived away and was last seen escaping 'at rooftop height'.

Fifteen minutes later, McKay sighted another two-seater over Passchendaele and, under fire from the enemy gunner, got under its tail and opened fire at 20 yards. The target, identified as a Junkers J-1*, dived straight into the ground. A month later, the same pilot shot down two D.F.W.s near Gheluvelt by zooming up under the tail of each without being sighted.

* J-I was one of the pioneer all-metal aircraft, a heavily-armoured contact patrol two-seat biplane which was very new to the Western Front at that time—the first having been assembled in October 1917—Editor.

In March 1918, a German offensive broke through the Allied front near St. Quentin and the squadron made a rapid series of moves to the rear as German infantry neared their airfields. Every available fighter was pressed into service attacking the advancing enemy until a line held near Amiens. At the end of April, No. 23 moved to St. Omer to re-equip with Sopwith Dolphins.

The Dolphin was a compact fighter powered, like the Spads, with a Hispano-Suiza engine. It was unusual in having back-staggered wings and the top mainplane was placed directly above the pilot. The upper wing was, however, low enough for the pilot to be able to see through the uncovered centre-section and compared to many fighters he had an excellent field of view. Twin Vickers guns were fitted and provision was made for a pair of Lewis guns to be carried on the top wing, making the Dolphin the most heavily-armed fighter available. In France, only one Lewis was normally fitted and even this was frequently removed since it tended to move during violent manoeuvres and the pilots preferred to use their twin Vickers and dispense with the weight of the Lewis.

At first, the back-staggered wings caused doubt among squadron pilots about handling qualities but the Dolphin was soon found to be reliable and handy. Other disadvantages were never overcome, notably the risk of head injuries should the aircraft overturn on landing and the mass of gun butts and struts hemming the pilot in.

During the summer of 1918, several other German offensives tried to break the Allies but it was the enemy's last effort. In August the German line broke and a retreat began. Throughout this period, No. 23's Dolphins were engaged in attacking enemy troops wherever found and there was relatively little air combat. Despite their low-level preoccupation, sufficient encounters with enemy fighters resulted in heavy losses to the enemy and a building-up of confidence in the ability of the Dolphins. Though few in number, they proved to be one of the best fighters of the war.

With the end of the war, No. 23 joined many others in being reduced to a cadre unit and moved back to England in March 1919. After spending the rest of the year at Waddington (Lincolnshire) the squadron was disbanded on the last day of 1919.

As part of the expanding home defence fighter force, No. 23 Squadron was re-formed at Henlow (Bedfordshire) on 1 July 1925. As interim equipment, some war-vintage, rotary-engined Sopwith Snipe and Avro 504Ks were issued and Squadron Leader Ray Collishaw arrived from No. 6 Group headquarters to command, bringing with him a reputation as one of the outstanding fighter pilots of the First World War.

1 Mixed formation No. 23 Squadron Bulldogs and Harts in 1932. (*Photo: Flt. Int. 12410.*)

2 Flight of Hart Fighters, three of a batch of six built for fighter trials which resulted in the Demon being placed in production. (*Photo: Flt. Int. 12401.*)

3 Blenheim Fighter running-up at Wittering January 1940 shows squadron's wartime code letters 'YP'. Camouflage for night fighting almost obliterated serial numbers. Note four-gun tray under fuselage. (*Photo: M.O.D. H.905.*)

4 Demon K5698 was fitted with a Frazer Nash 'turtle-back' turret for the rear gunner; the squadron's eagle emblem is contained in a spear-head frame used by fighter squadrons; bomber squadrons used a grenade-shaped frame. (*Photo: M.O.D. H.908.*)

5 The Commanding Officer's Turret Demon, Northolt 1937. The aerial array between wings and rudder would have been vulnerable to fire from turret in action. (*Photo: M.O.D. H.916.*)

6 Havoc BD121 is of the Intruder Mark I version with glazed nose. Most night fighting Havocs had solid noses mounting 8 or 12 machine guns. Note flare dampers below engines. This aircraft served with No. 23 Squadron from April till September 1941. (*Photo: I.W.M. CH2786.*)

In May 1926, new equipment arrived in the shape of Gloster Gamecocks and No. 23 said farewell to the rotary engine.

Routine training for a fighter squadron went on, with occasional visits to the gunnery training camp at Sutton Bridge (Lincolnshire) to fire at targets over The Wash. One diversion occurred in December 1928 when the current Commanding Officer, Squadron Leader A. G. Jones-Williams, was nominated as pilot for an attempt on the world distance record. His aircraft was to be the special Fairey long-range Monoplane (J9479) with a range of over 5,000 miles. On 24 April 1929, he and his navigator, Flight Lieutenant N. H. Jenkins left Cranwell (Lincolnshire) at 10:37 and landed at Karachi at 13:00 GMT on 26 April, a distance of 4,130 miles in 50 hours 37 minutes. It did not break the world record but was the first direct flight from England to India.

During 1931 several changes took place which were to have a far-reaching effect on the squadron's future history. In April, two flights were re-equipped with Bristol Bulldogs and, on July 10, a Hawker Hart was received. The Hart day-bomber had recently come into service and was currently outpacing most of the defending fighters. It appeared to be the ideal basis for a two-seat fighter, a class which had been extinct since the war. No. 23 was chosen to operate a flight of

1

4

2

5

3

6

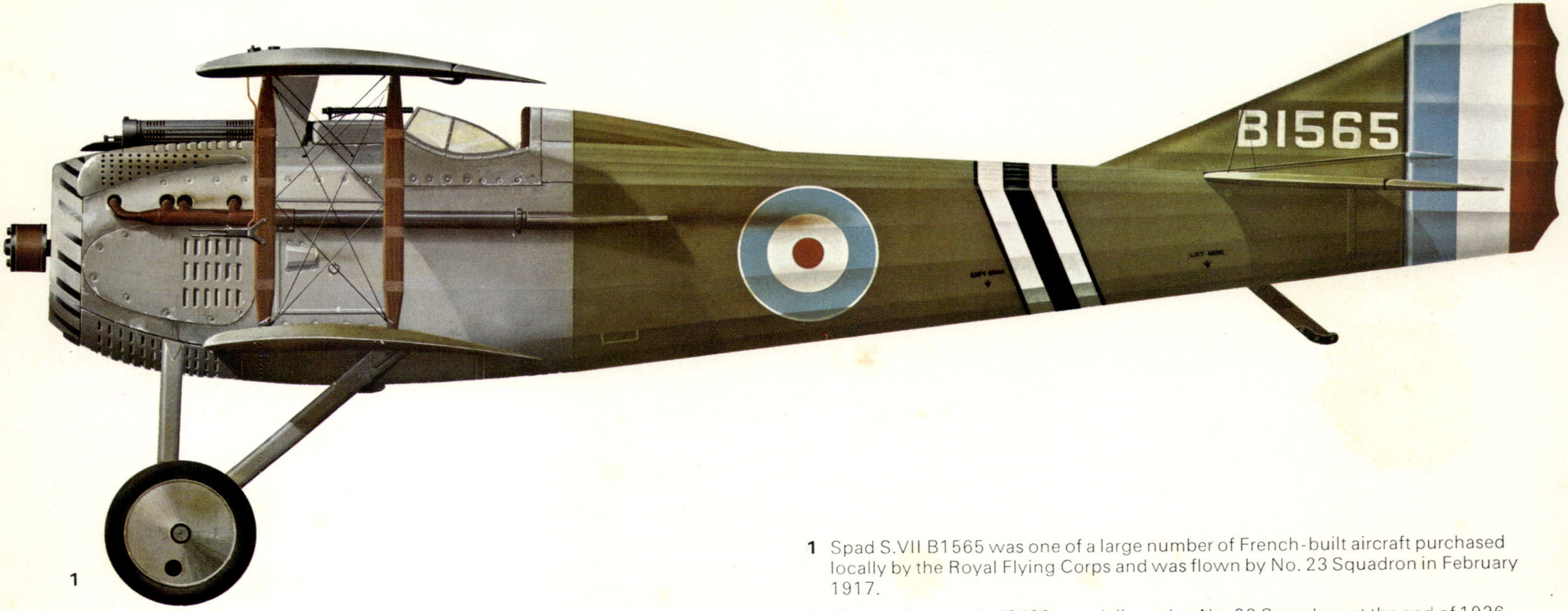

1

1 Spad S.VII B1565 was one of a large number of French-built aircraft purchased locally by the Royal Flying Corps and was flown by No. 23 Squadron in February 1917.

2 Gloster Gamecock J8409 was delivered to No. 23 Squadron at the end of 1926 and was one of the first aircraft to carry the squadron's eagle on the fin.

3 Douglas Havoc I Intruder BD121 served with No. 23 Squadron between April and September 1941, flying its last intruder mission on 16 September before being damaged in a flying accident two days later.

2

3

1

1 Gloster Javelin FAW.9 XH890 served with No. 23 Squadron between June 1960 and October 1964, when it was passed to No. 29 Squadron. After a heavy landing at Ndola, Zambia, on 2 June 1966, it was broken-up for spares.

2 De Havilland Mosquito II DZ228 was delivered to No. 23 Squadron on 8 December 1942 and was flown to Malta later in the month. It failed to return from its tenth operation, an intruder mission over Western Sicily, on 20 January 1943.

3 De Havilland Vampire NF.10 WP254 carried the code letter 'S' on its nose-wheel door. Delivered to No. 23 Squadron in December 1951, it was written-off in a crash on 16 August 1953.

2

3

Hart Fighters powered by a supercharged Kestrel engine and armed with a pair of Vickers guns for the pilot and a single Lewis for the gunner. The squadron flew as a composite unit proving the Hart Fighter which, in July 1932, was renamed Demon. By April 1933, No. 23 had converted entirely to two-seaters.

Many R.A.F. squadrons moved to the Middle East during the Abyssinian crisis of 1935/6 but No. 23 remained at home. Many of its pilots and aircraft were taken away to reinforce other squadrons destined for overseas so that by March 1936, the squadron had only one Demon left. Fortunately, at this point the trend was reversed and pilots and aircraft began to arrive to bring it once more up to full strength.

The excellent performance of the two-motor Bristol Blenheim medium-bomber made it eligible for consideration as a fighter. Demons were obsolescent but, since Demon squadrons had trained gunners, they were the logical units to receive Blenheim Fighters. Early in December 1938, No. 23 began converting to twin engines, retractable undercarriages, enclosed cockpits and gun turrets. Several were lost in accidents including one on 20 July 1939, when Sergeant J. A. Bullard was carrying a cadet from Oundle School as passenger. The aircraft went out of control and Bullard pushed the boy clear of the crashing aircraft to safety but sacrificed his own chance to parachute by doing so.

On the outbreak of World War Two, No. 23 was allocated to night defence and dispersed its aircraft around Wittering (Northamptonshire). On 30 October 1939, the squadron flew its first real operation by putting up Red and Yellow Sections to cover a force of Royal Navy destroyers 150 miles out into the North Sea. Though several aircraft were sighted, all turned out to be R.A.F. Blenheims or Hudsons. Patrols over lightships and convoys became commonplace.

The Battle of France brought increasing German activity over England and the squadron met the *Luftwaffe* in force for the first time on 18 June 1940. Seven Blenheims were on night patrol and three intercepted enemy aircraft. Sergeant Close radioed that he was chasing an enemy (an He 111) but as he approached from astern a burst of fire shattered the glass nose and killed him. His gunner, Leading Aircraftman Karasek, succeeded in parachuting before the Blenheim crashed in flames. Pilot Officer R. M. Duke-Woolley witnessed the event from near King's Lynn (Norfolk) and chased the enemy bomber. After firing two bursts into it, an engine caught fire and the Heinkel crashed at Cley-on-Sea near Sheringham (Norfolk), the crew of four being taken prisoner. The Blenheim returned to Wittering with one engine out of action.

Squadron Leader J. O'Brien's target was first seen held by searchlights near Newmarket (Suffolk). Getting below the enemy permitted Corporal Little to fire several bursts from the dorsal turret and the bomber turned to port and dived, giving O'Brien a chance with the front guns—four 0·303-in. Brownings in a ventral tray. Smoke came from the starboard engine and the He 111 dived away to crash near Newmarket. The Blenheim overshot and suddenly went into an uncontrollable spin. O'Brien ordered his crew to abandon the aircraft but the gunner failed to get clear of his turret while the navigator was struck by a propeller and killed. The pilot landed safely by parachute but a second Blenheim had been lost.

It was obvious that the Blenheim was not the most suitable aircraft for night fighting. It was too slow, the armament was too light to have a decisive effect in the short time available and the type was vulnerable to return fire from the enemy. Primitive radar sets were gradually fitted but were still experimental. Other squadrons began to receive heavily-armed and much faster Bristol Beaufighters but No. 23 was not on the list for re-equipment.

In the absence of methods of finding enemy bombers easily while they were over Britain, it was decided that one certain spot to find an enemy bomber was over its base. During December, the squadron stood by to intrude over Northern France where it was hoped the Blenheim crews would be able to locate the airfields from which German bombers operated and attack them as they came in to land. On 21 December, six Blenheims set off on patrols over the Abbeville/Amiens/Poix areas. Seven more went out on the following night; none sighted an enemy aircraft but one Blenheim had to be abandoned as fuel ran out over the Isle of Wight.

On the second day of 1941, at last, No. 23 achieved success. Flying Officer P. S. B. Ensor took 'U-for-Uncle' to the vicinity of Caen and sighted an aircraft with its navigation lights on. He trailed it to Dreux where he decided to attack as fuel was running short. Opening fire at 100 yards he saw an explosion near the tail of the quarry, now identified as a He 111. Taken by surprise near its own base, the enemy bomber fired a recognition cartridge, apparently assuming that the attack was carried out by a German fighter in error. Ensor attacked again but ran out of ammunition after 3 seconds and had to watch the Heinkel dive away, apparently out of control.

In March 1941, a new type was received. Several Douglas Boston light-bombers had been converted to night-fighters by the addition of forward-firing guns. These were more modern than the Blenheims and gradually replaced them, though not before the latter had claimed a final enemy aircraft. On 21 April, Flight Lieutenant B. R. O'Bryen-Hoare took off from Manston (Kent) in 'T-for-Tommy' en route for Achiet airfield. Seeing Douai illuminated, he dropped four 40-lb bombs across the flare path and all lights went out immediately. St. Leger airfield was similarly bright and the navigation lights of two circling aircraft were seen. The first landed before the Blenheim arrived but O'Bryen-Hoare got behind the second which fired its recognition cartridge. Opening fire from 50 yards astern, the enemy was seen to be a large four-engined aircraft* which exploded and fell in pieces. The Blenheim returned with parts of the enemy aircraft embedded in its wing.

Douglas Havocs—the name adopted by the R.A.F. for this version of the Boston—began flying intruder missions on 7 April when Wing Commander G. F. W. Heycock, No. 23's Commanding Officer, took AW404 over France. Every bomber airfield in an arc from Gilze-Rijen in The Netherlands to Caen in Normandy was visited during the following months. During May 1941, six attacks were made on aircraft over their bases and the number increased as experience was gained. On 13 August, Pilot Officer W. A. Bird took 'B-for-Beer' into the circuit at Gilze-Rijen to attack fleeting targets seven times, finishing his sortie, dropping 18 × 40-lb bombs and 60 incendiaries on dispersal areas.

Early in 1942, Havocs were supplemented by Boston IIIs capable of carrying four 250-lb bombs.

In July 1942, de Havilland Mosquitos began to arrive. These wooden aircraft had a maximum speed of 370 m.p.h. and a fixed armament of four 20-mm cannon and four 0·303-in machine-guns. Powered by two Rolls-Royce Merlins, the Mosquito was the most effective intruder aircraft of the war. The crew consisted of pilot and navigator so once more the squadron posted its gunners, on this occasion for the last time. Wing Commander O'Bryen-Hoare opened its career with No. 23 by taking a Mosquito II 'S-for-Sugar' to Etampes where a Dornier Do 217 was shot down. Two nights later, Squadron Leader K. H. Salisbury-Hughes took the same 'S-for-Sugar' back to Etampes and destroyed another Do 217, returning by Evreux where a He 111 was attacked. The resulting explosion threw the Mosquito on to its back.

When no *Luftwaffe* aircraft could be found, trains and barges came under attack. No radar was allowed to be carried to prevent capture should a Mosquito intruder land intact in enemy territory. Operating at night over blacked-out countryside presented hazards for crews and losses from *flak* and night fighters could be expected. On the night of 8 August, for example, five Mosquitos

* Probably an anti-shipping Focke-Wulf FW 200 Condor—Editor.

1

2

3

4

5

6

1 A trio of black Havocs of No. 23 Squadron. (*Photo: I.W.M. CH2787.*)

2 A formation of Vampire NF.10s over Norfolk. (*Photo: Flight International 28084.*)

3 Mosquito DZ228 flying over Malta in desert camouflage in December 1942. It was lost in action a few weeks later. (*Photo: I.W.M. CM4658A.*)

4 A Mosquito Mk. VI fighter-bomber in Sicily in the autumn of 1943. HJ675 was posted missing from an intruder mission on 15 January 1944. (*Photo: No. 23 Squadron archives.*)

5 Mosquito NF.36 RL264 'YP-D' at Lubeck, Germany in August 1947. (*Photo: No. 23 Squadron archives.*)

6 No. 23 Squadron Vampire NF.10s lined up at Coltishall; some carry the squadron badge on the nose and all have squadron markings on the tail booms. (*Photo: Flight International 28083.*)

1

2

went out on patrol and three failed to return—reasons unknown. Fortunately this was uncommon and losses were low for the rest of the year.

In December 1942, the squadron was posted overseas. Long-range tanks were fitted and the aircraft painted in a new camouflage scheme ready for the flight to Malta. Ground crews left by sea on 10 December and, on 21 December, the aircraft flew to Portreath (Cornwall), jumping-off point for flights to Gibraltar and beyond. Good weather forecast for the route allowed 17 Mosquitos to leave on 23 December, all arriving safely at Gibraltar though one was damaged on landing. Then, on 29 December, Wing Commander Peter Wykeham-Barnes led the first flight of six to Malta. Operations over Sicily began two days later when the C.O. and a Rhodesian, Pilot Officer Williams, flew DZ230 and DZ234 on intruder sorties.

From Malta, targets in Tunisia and Sicily were within range. Road convoys of the retreating *Afrika Korps* were attacked in Southern Tunisia. Soon, trains in Southern Italy also came under attack. During the last full month before the end of the campaign in North Africa, the squadron flew 105 sorties, destroying four enemy aircraft, damaging four more and shooting-up 15 trains. Six Mosquitos were lost during the month.

In July 1943, the Allied armies were to land in Sicily and the task of the Malta-based fighters was to secure air superiority over the area. No. 23's contribution was to make the use of Sicilian airfields as hazardous as possible and in fact few enemy aircraft were to be found by the time the invasion force went ashore. Some Mark VI Mosquito fighter-bombers were received which could carry a pair of 250-lb bombs on wing racks and two more in the bomb-bay. Later this war-load was doubled (500-lb bombs) and the Mark VIs spent much of their effort attacking railway yards and transformer stations in an attempt to hamper enemy supplies and reinforcements.

The Mosquito's speed and handling qualities brought confidence to No. 23's crews. Flight Sergeant P. Rudd and Sergeant Messingham were returning from Taranto in DZ706 low over the sea when an enemy aircraft passed overhead. Turning tightly, the Mosquito climbed after what was now recognizable as an Me 210 fighter-bomber and slowly overtook it. A short burst caused smoke to pour out of the starboard engine. The Messerschmitt dived to sea-level with return fire coming from its remotely-controlled barbettes on the fuselage sides. Just above the sea, the Me 210 made a steep turn but the Mosquito succeeded in turning even more tightly and scored hits with several bursts. So tight was the turn that the Mosquito stalled and nearly hit the water before recovering. The enemy was nowhere to be seen from sea-level and was presumed to have plunged into the water.

On 1 September 1943, the squadron flew its 1,000th sortie from Malta. Twenty-three enemy aircraft had been destroyed and a similar number damaged. Over 300 attacks had been made on ground targets for the loss of 16 Mosquitos on operations and three in accidents.

During December, No. 23 moved to Sardinia which brought Southern France into range. Shipping, trains and road transport were attacked from Montpellier to the Po valley. In April 1944 the squadron concentrated on communications leading north from Rome to prepare for its capture by Allied troops and this marked the end of operations in the Mediterranean. On 5 May orders came for the transfer of the squadron back to Britain. Three days later, the Mosquitos were flown to Algiers and on 19 May the crews embarked in the *Mooltan* and joined a convoy that included the *Strathnaver* with No. 23's ground crews. On 28 May, the Clyde was reached and after four days at anchor all personnel were disembarked and moved by train to Norfolk.

Despite its soporific name, Little Snoring (not far from Fakenham, Norfolk) echoed to the sound of Merlins day and night. No. 100 Group was responsible for countering enemy attempts to stop the R.A.F. night bomber offensive which was reducing Germany's war potential to rubble. The Group's Mosquito squadrons had two main tasks—attacking enemy night-fighters lying in wait for the bomber stream and, also, intruding over enemy airfields to restrict the operation of night-fighters and harass them on take-off and landing. No. 23's role was designated as low-level intruding, and missions began on 6 July. Few enemy aircraft were seen in the air but successful attacks were carried out on airfields and trains for the rest of the month.

Early in August, a change from night sorties came when the squadron joined No. 515 in providing escorts for a daylight raid by Avro Lancasters on Bordeaux. Thirteen aircraft from each squadron accompanied the heavy-bombers all the way back from the target, repeating the operation on the following day. Other daylight operations included escorting Boeing Fortresses of No. 214 Squadron operating radar counter-measures equipment and providing cover for Lancasters bombing Bergen in Norway.

No. 23's Mosquitos lost their nose machine-guns to make room for ASH, the American-built A.I.Mk.XV radar and intensive training with the new equipment continued during December. Meanwhile, standard Mosquitos ranged over Northern Europe.

Despite its wooden construction, the Mosquito could absorb considerable punishment and still stay airborne. Flight Lieutenant D. L. Badley, a Royal New Zealand Air Force officer, and Flight Sergeant A. A. Wilson had reason to be grateful for this ability after a lengthy trip in PZ458 to Copenhagen. Over Vaerlose airfield, they attacked several light-grey Junkers Ju 88s and hit three. But PZ458 suffered strikes from the intense *flak*. The port engine, bomb-bay, rear fuselage and hydraulics were damaged and the engine had to be shut down. Radio and rudder trim refused to function but the Mosquito brought its crew back across the North Sea to a belly-landing at Woodbridge (Suffolk) emergency landing ground without injury to the crew.

Intruder flights reached as far as Austria and in April 1945 the squadron took on a new task. No. 23 joined Nos. 141 and 515 Squadrons in attacks on enemy airfields which were first marked by target indicators and then bombed. Eighty 4-lb incendiaries were carried except when flares were accommodated and Riem and Neubiberg airfields (near Munich) were the first targets. On 2 May the squadron flew its last operation when it joined No. 141 Squadron in attacks on Hohn and Flensburg (on the Baltic near the Danish frontier) airfields.

During August, a few Mosquito Mk. 30s arrived to replace the Mark VIs but warning of disbandment arrived before conversion. On 25 September, the squadron was disbanded and the Mosquitos ferried to West Freugh and Kirkbride.

As one of the longest-serving squadrons of the R.A.F., No. 23 was selected to form part of the post-war establishment. On 11 September 1946, it reformed at Wittering as a night-fighter squadron, armed with the faithful Mosquito. The marks in use were the NF.30 and NF.36, both of which carried A.I. radar in a bulged

1 Venom NF.3 all-weather fighters over the Norfolk coast. (*Photo: Flight International 32918.*)

2 No. 23 Sqdn's Venom NF.2s carried squadron badge just forward of cockpit and squadron markings on tail booms. (*Photo: M.O.D. PRB7551.*)

3 A pair of Javelin FAW.7s carrying D.H. Firestreak missiles. (*Photo: M.O.D. PRB218035.*)

4 No. 23 Squadron's Javelin FAW.4s lined up at Horsham St Faith 1957. Red eagle emblem on fin is lost on camouflage and squadron markings above serial number on engine intakes is similarly indistinct. (*Photo: Aeroplane No. 17867.*)

3

4

1 The squadron's Javelin T.3 trainer displays eagle on white background and squadron marking outlined in white to improve presentation. XH432 served with squadron for four years from April 1959. (*Photo: Peter M. Corbell.*)

2 August 1964, No. 23 Sqdn began to convert to Lightnings, one of its first new aircraft formates with Javelin FAW.9 XH886. Note 'two-tone' eagle emblem. (*Photo: M.O.D. PRB 28777.*)

3 A Firestreak-armed Javelin FAW.9 of No. 23 Sqdn, XH793 served with squadron between April 1960-March 1964. Note reheat nozzles which marked difference between FAW.7 and FAW.9. (*Photo: M.O.D. PRB 22307.*)

4 Javelin XH887 takes on fuel from a Valiant tanker of No. 214 Squadron through its refuelling probe. (*Photo: M.O.D. PRB 19707.*)

nose and were armed with four 20-mm cannon. These served for five years before a replacement arrived.

The need for faster night-fighters had been foreseen and a two-seat night fighter variant of the Meteor jet fighter was under development. The Korean war which had broken out in September 1950 had given a new urgency to air defence and, to supplement the Meteors, the Air Ministry took delivery of a night-fighter version of the de Havilland Vampire which had been developed as a private venture. An order by Egypt had been embargoed because of the Arab/Israeli conflict and the aircraft taken over by the R.A.F. as the Vampire NF.10. In September 1951 the first of No. 23's aircraft arrived but delivery was slow and by January 1952 only seven aircraft were on strength.

The Vampire's speed of 550 m.p.h. and easy handling made it far more effective than the wartime Mosquitos, the armament remaining as four 20-mm cannon. No. 23 covered the East Coast from its base at Coltishall (Norfolk) and crews found the Vampire pleasant to fly. Its only accidents came in an unlucky spell between May and August 1953 when three were lost in accidents. On 25 November 1953, the first Venom NF.2 arrived at Coltishall, by January 1954 conversion was complete.

Though similar in layout to the Vampire, the Venom night-fighter was much faster, being capable of 630 m.p.h. in its final form. By the end of 1955, 16 were in service with the squadron which was the first to be equipped with the type. Venom NF.3s gradually replaced the earlier mark from October 1955 onwards, being fitted with improved radar and power controls.

Replacement of the Venom began in April 1957 when four Gloster Javelin FAW.4s were delivered. Powered by two Sapphire engines, the Javelin was a large delta-winged all-weather fighter which was supersonic in a dive and had a ceiling of over 50,000 feet. Its nose radar was more effective than earlier types and later versions were equipped with air-to-air missiles. The armament of four 30-mm Aden cannon was heavier than any previously used on night-fighters. Missile-equipped Mark 7s began to arrive in April 1959 and completely replaced the earlier version by July. Two, XH781 and XH775 were lost in a collision over Brundall (Norfolk) on 1 September 1959. These were the only two to be destroyed in accidents for the rest of the Javelin's service with the squadron, though a Mark 9 (XH845) was accidentally burnt-out on the ground at Leuchars (Fifeshire) in August 1964. The Javelin FAW.9s were modified FAW.7s and carried long refuelling booms for air-to-air refuelling.

During March 1963, the squadron moved to Leuchars in Scotland where, in August 1964, it started to receive English Electric Lightnings. As these were single-seat all-weather fighters, No. 23 lost its navigators. Armed with a pair of air-to-air missiles, Lightnings have a top speed of about 1,500 m.p.h.

The main task of No. 23's Lightnings is the interception and identification of aircraft approaching the U.K. but the ability of the Lightning to use air-refuelling means that it can be deployed quickly to overseas bases.

The squadron's red eagle emblem has been seen in Canada after a non-stop flight from Leuchars to Toronto by a pair of Lightning F.6s. In an age where mobility is at a premium, doubtless it will continue to be seen far from the squadron's Scottish base.

SQUADRON BASES

Gosport, Hampshire	1 September 1915
Fienvillers, France	16 March 1916
Le Hameau, France	18 March 1916
Fienvillers, France	1 September 1916
Vert Galand, France	5 September 1916
Baizieux, France	5 March 1917
Auchel, France	23 May 1917
Bruay, France	29 May 1917
La Lovie, France	13 June 1917
Matigny, France	16 February 1918
Moreuil, France	22 March 1918
Bertangles, France	28 March 1918
St. Omer, France	29 April 1918
Bertangles, France	16 May 1918
Cappy, France	13 September 1918
Hancourt, France	11 October 1918
Bertry East, France	25 October 1918
Clermont, France	3 December 1918
Waddington, Lincolnshire	15 March 1919 to 31 December 1919
Henlow, Bedfordshire	1 July 1925
Kenley, Surrey	6 February 1927
Biggin Hill, Kent	17 September 1932
Northolt, Middlesex	21 December 1936
Wittering, Northamptonshire	16 May 1938
Collyweston, Northamptonshire	31 May 1940
Ford, Sussex	12 September 1940
Middle Wallop, Hampshire	Det. 12 September 1940 to 25 September 1940
Manston, Kent	6 August 1942
Bradwell Bay, Essex	14 August 1942
Manston, Kent	21 August 1942
Bradwell Bay, Essex	13 October 1942
Ground echelon embarked for Malta	11 December 1942
Portreath, Cornwall	21 December 1942*
Gibraltar	23 December 1942*
Luqa, Malta	27 December 1942*
Sigonella, Sicily	Det. 3 September 1943 to 5 October 1943
Gerbini Main, Sicily	Det. 5 October 1943 to 1 November 1943
Pomigliano, Italy	Det. 1 November 1943 to 7 December 1943
Alghero, Sardinia	7 December 1943
Blida, Algeria	8 May 1944*
Embarked for U.K.	19 May 1944
Little Snoring, Norfolk	2 June 1944 to 25 September 1945
Wittering, Northamptonshire	11 September 1946
Coltishall, Norfolk	23 January 1947
Church Fenton, Yorkshire	19 November 1949
Coltishall, Norfolk	22 September 1950
Horsham St. Faith, Norfolk	15 January 1952
Coltishall, Norfolk	4 July 1952
Horsham St. Faith, Norfolk	12 October 1956
Coltishall, Norfolk	28 May 1957
Leuchars, Fifeshire	9 March 1963 completed by 21 March 1963

* Air echelon only

SQUADRON EQUIPMENT Period of Use & Typical Serial and Code Letters

Aircraft	Period of Use	Typical Serial and Code Letters
Avro 504A	September 1915 to March 1916	4024
Bleriot XI	September 1915 to October 1915	574
Caudron G.III	September 1915 to December 1915	5270
Maurice Farman	September 1915 to January 1916	2947
Martinsyde S.1	October 1915 to March 1916	4251
B.E.2c	October 1915 to March 1916	2048
F.E.2b	January 1916 to February 1917	5208
Spad S.VII (& S.XIII)	February 1917 to April 1918	B6840 (M)
Sopwith Dolphin	March 1918 to March 1919	E4729 (P)
Sopwith Snipe	July 1925 to May 1926	E6340
Gloster Gamecock I	April 1926 to September 1931	J8041
Bristol Bulldog IIA	April 1931 to April 1933	K1672
Hawker Hart (F) & Demon	July 1931 to December 1938	K5698 (MS-G)
Bristol Blenheim IF	December 1938 to April 1941	L8655 (YP-E)
Douglas Havoc I	March 1941 to August 1942	BD121 (YP-F)
Douglas Boston III	February 1942 to August 1942	W8283
de Havilland Mosquito II	July 1942 to September 1943	DD795 (YP-J)
de Havilland Mosquito VI	May 1943 to September 1945	HJ737 (YP-R)
de Havilland Mosquito NF.30	August 1945 to September 1945	
	September 1946 to February 1947	NT326
de Havilland Mosquito NF.36	February 1947 to May 1952	RL193 (YP-B)
de Havilland Vampire NF.10	September 1951 to January 1954	WP248 (B)
de Havilland Venom NF.2	November 1953 to March 1956	WL821 (A)
de Havilland Venom NF.3	October 1955 to May 1957	WX803
Gloster Javelin FAW.4	April 1957 to July 1959	XA737
Gloster Javelin FAW.7	April 1959 to July 1960	XH849 (C)
Gloster Javelin FAW.9	April 1960 to September 1964	XH845 (N)
English Electric Lightning F.3	August 1964 to November 1967	XP760 (K)
English Electric Lightning F.6	May 1967 to date	XR763 (G)

COMMANDING OFFICERS

Captain (later Major) L.A.Strange	1 September 1915
Major R.E.T.Hogg	22 January 1916
Major A.Ross-Hume	24 April 1916
Major G.B.J.Leighton MC	21 January 1917
Major A.M.Wilkinson DSO	10 May 1917
Major E.O.Grenfell MC	31 August 1917
Major C.E.Bryant DSO	28 October 1917
S/Ldr. R.Collishaw DSO, OBE DSC, DFC	1 July 1925
S/Ldr. A.G.Jones-Williams MC	21 January 1928
S/Ldr. H.W.Woollett DSO, MC	15 January 1930
S/Ldr. A.L.Paxton DFC	28 December 1931
S/Ldr. H.G.Crowe MC	16 February 1933
S/Ldr. G.V.Howard DFC	1 September 1935
S/Ldr. R.Y.Eccles	16 November 1936
S/Ldr. V.B.J.Jackson	22 May 1939
S/Ldr. C.E.Beamish	4 October 1939
S/Ldr. L.C.Bicknell	18 January 1940
S/Ldr. G.F.W.Heycock	8 August 1940
S/Ldr. C.H.A.Colman	25 November 1940
W/Cdr. G.F.W.Heycock	4 January 1941
W/Cdr. R.H.A.Leigh	10 May 1941
W/Cdr. W.J.Crisham	8 December 1941
W/Cdr. B.R.O' Bryen-Hoare DFC	17 April 1942
W/Cdr. P.Wykeham-Barnes DSO, DFC	23 September 1942
W/Cdr. J.B.Selby DSO, DFC	25 April 1943
W/Cdr. P.R.Burton-Giles DSO, DFC	5 September 1943
W/Cdr. A.M.Murphy DSO, DFC, C. de G.	10 December 1943
W/Cdr. S.P.Russell DFC	2 December 1944
S/Ldr. P.G.K.Williamson DFC	1 September 1946
S/Ldr. D.L.Norris-Smith	21 July 1947
S/Ldr. V.S.H.Duclos DFC	17 October 1949
S/Ldr. A.J.Jacomb-Hood DFC	17 December 1951
S/Ldr. M.H.Constable-Maxwell DSO, DFC	22 January 1954
S/Ldr. P.S.Engelbach	3 May 1954
S/Ldr. C.R.Winter DFC	15 February 1955
W/Cdr. A.N.Davis DSO, DFC	21 July 1955
W/Cdr. J.E.Kilduff	1 August 1957
W/Cdr. G.I.Chapman AFC	22 July 1959
W/Cdr. D.B.Wills DFC	30 June 1961
W/Cdr. A.J.Owen DFC, AFC, DFM	17 May 1962
S/Ldr. J.MacLeod	1 October 1964
W/Cdr. K.A.Williamson AFC	16 June 1966
W/Cdr. D.McClen	5 July 1968
W/Cdr. R.D.Stone AFC	8 May 1970

No.29 Squadron

D.H.2s of No. 29 Squadron at their airfield at Abeele, near Ypres. Their hangar accommodation was more permanent than usually found on Royal Flying Corps airfields, which were normally equipped with transportable hangars. (*Photo: Ministry of Defence H.1925.*)

By the end of the first year of World War One, it had become apparent that reconnaissance—the main task of the Royal Flying Corps—was not being carried out without increasing opposition from the enemy not only on the ground but in the air. From the first desultory engagements involving such unsuitable weapons as revolvers and automatic rifles—even shotguns—there evolved the real menace of the fast single-seater 'scout' armed with a machine-gun. The ultimate development was to be the synchronization gear which permitted the pilot to fire through the propeller arc. In other words, he could 'aim' his aircraft directly at the enemy and dispense with the difficult deflection shooting necessary with machine-guns awkwardly mounted to clear the propeller disc. The first step towards synchronized interrupter gear was ingeniously simple. Toughened steel deflector plates were fitted to the wooden propeller blades. Thus, those bullets which did not clear the fast revolving blades would be deflected off the plates.

To counter the enemy's new hostile advantage, R.F.C. squadrons formed for fighting purposes only were equipped and sent to France. These replaced the small number of single-seat scouts flown by the reconnaissance squadrons and No. 29 was the second D.H.2 unit.

Formed at Gosport (Hampshire) on 7 November 1915, a nucleus—supplied by No. 23 Squadron—trained with Avro 504as, Caudron G.IIIs and B.E.s until March 1916 when No. 29 began to receive its first D.H.2 fighters. This was a 28-ft. span twin-boom pusher biplane powered by a 100 h.p. Gnome rotary mounted behind the pilot. The engine's pusher position allowed—in the absence of a British interrupter gear—a Lewis gun to be mounted in front of the pilot and firing dead ahead. At first this was on a movable mount but was later fixed to a rigid mounting for easier aiming. The top speed was only 93 m.p.h. at low altitudes but the D.H.2 was manoeuvrable and well-built, if difficult to fly.

On 25 March, No. 29 Squadron left for France. Ten D.H.2s headed for Dover but encountered a snowstorm and six aircraft force-landed, two-thirds being wrecked. Two more D.H.2s joined the squadron at Dover and four crossed the Channel to St. Omer where one crashed on landing. To compound the misfortunes of the new squadron, the ground personnel became involved in an outbreak of measles and were quarantined at Rouen. Finally on 15 April, 10 D.H.2s were flown to their operational base at Abeele, near Ypres.

Patrols over the lines began and the D.H.2s of Nos. 24 and 29 Squadrons, supplemented in May by No. 32 Squadron, succeeded in earning a respite for the hard-pressed reconnaissance biplanes which successfully photographed the enemy lines in preparation for the Battle of the Somme. On the first day of the battle, enemy observation balloons were attacked while fighter patrols kept enemy reconnaissance aircraft away.

Occasional encounters resulted in the destruction of a number of Fokker E.III monoplane scouts and German reconnaissance aircraft found near the lines. The first to fall to the guns of the squadron was a two-seater attacked on 1 May by Lieutenant H. O. D. Segrave (who was later to become famous as a holder of both the world land and water speed records as Sir Henry Segrave).

Another famous pilot joined No. 29 in August 1916. He was Sergeant James McCudden who was destined to destroy over 50 enemy aircraft before his death in an accident in 1918 after being awarded the Victoria Cross. On 6 September, he was flying D.H.2 No. 5985 when a white Albatros was seen over Messines. After two drums had been expended on it, the German aircraft dived away steeply. No claim was made for its destruction but Australian troops near Ypres saw it crash not far from the Menin Road. McCudden shot down four more before leaving the squadron.

Already the D.H.2s were being outclassed by the new Albatros fighters organized into fighting units manned by picked pilots. Losses mounted and it was obvious that a replacement was overdue. On 11 March 1917, six Nieuport 17s arrived and the last D.H.2s were withdrawn from service on 21 March and flown away to the depot. As the Commanding Officer, Major W. A. Gratton-Bellew took off in A2572, the engine stopped and the aircraft crashed, fatally injuring the pilot.

The Nieuports which No. 29 received were highly popular with the squadron pilots. Their agility, speed and rate of climb were appreciated by men who had spent the last six months flying inferior-performance aircraft. The summer of 1917 was to see the arrival in numbers of Pups, Camels, S.E.5s and Bristol Fighters which were to provide the R.F.C. with mastery of the air over the front line a year later.

The Third Battle of Ypres in July 1917 brought heavy fighting in the air above the battered town. On 12 July, the largest air battle to date found Captain S. P. Simpson in B1617 and Lieutenant Miller (B1506) involved in a dogfight between about 14 enemy

fighters and patrols of Pups and S.E.5s. They accounted for three of the enemy which fell to the ground out of control. Second Lieutenant D. F. Hilton had a contrary effect on an observation balloon near Polygon Wood. Hilton's Nieuport (B3494) was one of a patrol of five which attacked balloons and his target, instead of falling to earth, promptly ascended rapidly as the observer took to his parachute. Apparently a bullet had severed the mooring cable and Hilton chased the runaway to 18,000 feet before getting it to catch fire. Later he attacked an Albatros flying at 500 feet and sent it down to crash near Westhoek.

Low-flying attacks on enemy troops and transport behind the lines was another task undertaken by No. 29 from time to time. Though effective, it exposed the wood and fabric fighters to small-arms fire from the ground, making such activities hazardous. Reprisals from the enemy in the form of a night-bombing attack on Poperinghe aerodrome resulted in the death of the Commanding Officer, Major C. M. B. Chapman and four others on 1 November.

During April 1918, the squadron moved to Teteghem (near Dunkirk) and gave up its Nieuports for S.E.5as. On 15 May, the new fighters destroyed their first enemy when Captain R. H. Rusby flying D5963 attacked two German two-seaters near Merris and shot one down in flames. Captain H. G. White (in D3942) dived on a Pfalz on 19 May and in pulling out after firing 50 rounds collided with it. The enemy fighter rolled over the top of the S.E. and went down vertically whereupon White dived after it firing. The Pfalz lost its wings and the S.E.'s engine stopped leaving the pilot to crash-land his almost-uncontrollable aircraft.

As the war neared its end, larger formations of aircraft operated together. Day bombers were protected by squadrons of fighters and were opposed by fast new Fokker D.VIIs. On 12 August 1918, Captain C. H. R. Lagesse led a patrol of nine S.E.5as which encountered about 15 enemy aircraft. The British fighters attacked a squadron of eight Fokker D.VIIs and a Pfalz at 12,000 feet over Kemmel and a dogfight ensued which ended 10 minutes later at 300 feet over Comines.

1 The close resemblance of the F.E.8 to the D.H.2 is evident in this photograph of No. 7457. Note the flexible Lewis gun which could be secured when not in use. (*Photo: I.W.M. Q.66943.*)

2 A squadron Grebe at Northolt in 1926 fitted with racks for light bombs. (*Photo: Ministry of Defence H.570.*)

3 No. 29 Squadron's S.E.5as lined up at Oudezeele in August, 1918. Each aircraft carries its identification letter under the wing. (*Photo: I.W.M. Q.6060.*)

Lieutenant Dougan in D6947 saw the top wing of a D.VII which he attacked come off at 5,000 feet; Lieutenant Wareing (C1133) attacked the sole Pfalz whose wings folded up over Ploegsteert; Lieutenant Hoy (D6939) downed a D.VII near Comines and Lieutenant Ross (C9071) set fire to another. Lieutenant Venter (D6965) shot down one D.VII out of control and attacked a second which dived into the ground north-east of Armentières. No. 29's only casualty was Captain Davies who was wounded in the arm and crashed his S.E.5a (D6944) in his own lines. On the way home Lieutenant Harrison in E5947 shot down a kite balloon in flames near Estaires.

Later in the day, Lagesse and three other pilots encountered an equal number of D.VIIs and destroyed them all. A total of 42 aircraft and eight balloons were shot down during August and enemy opposition began to wane.

During October, low-flying attacks were carried out on railways and roads against the retreating German armies. A typical raid on Courtrai railway yards on 14 October dispensed thirty 25-lb bombs among trucks and railway coaches from 15 S.E.5as. Climbing away, the squadron encountered seven D.VIIs near Rouliers and shot down two. Fifteen minutes later 16 D.VIIs dived on the British fighters and 2 more were destroyed. Shortly after, five D.VIIs were spotted at 16,000 feet and attacked and one went down out of control while five D.F.W. two-seaters seen nearby lost one of their number. Lieutenant C. M. Wilson in F5516 was missing when the squadron reached home while Captain Lagesse in E4084 force-landed at La Lovie with his radiator shot through.

Within a few weeks, an armistice had been signed and silence fell over the battle areas. During December the squadron moved to an airfield near Cologne as part of the army of occupation where it stayed until reduced to a cadre in July 1919. In August it returned to the U.K. and remained at Spittlegate (Lincolnshire) until disbanded on 31 December 1919.

To swell the thin ranks of the fighter defences of the United Kingdom, No. 29 Squadron was reformed at Duxford (Cambridgeshire) on 1 April 1923. Its equipment was the wartime Sopwith Snipe powered by a Bentley rotary and it was January 1925 before a post-war type was obtained in the shape of Gloster Grebes.

In April 1928, a move was made to North Weald, a wartime airfield in Essex which had been rebuilt as one of the fighter stations guarding the eastern approaches to London. Armstrong Whitworth Siskins were received at the same time and an idea of the state of the air defences is given by the tactics adopted in air exercises. On occasions, the first intimation of an 'enemy' raid approaching London was the sighting of a gaggle of bombers from the squadron's airfield which necessitated a rapid take-off and pursuit. In June 1932, Bristol Bulldogs replaced the Siskins and radio-telegraphy became standard, enabling fighters to be directed by R/T from the ground and controlled by the formation leader.

In March 1935, the squadron was converted to a two-seat fighter unit, there being a school of thought in the R.A.F. that the ability to defend a fighter's tail was worth the extra weight of a gunner and his equipment. The success of the Bristol Fighters during the First World War lent weight to the argument and the availability of the Hawker Demon—a variant of the famous Hart series—meant that two-seaters had the same speed as Bulldogs. The change had a far-reaching effect on No. 29's future role.

A crisis had developed by Italy's action in invading Ethiopia and sanctions against the aggressor were proposed by the League of Nations. Much talk was expended but only Britain took any practical steps to back up the League's resolutions. R.A.F. squadrons in the Middle East were reinforced by home-based units and on 26 September, the squadron's Demons were flown to Sealand (Cheshire) for packing while the personnel embarked on the *Cameronian* at Liverpool on 4 October. Arriving at Alexandria on 13 October, both aircraft and personnel were sent to Amriya where the Demons, once re-assembled and rigged, stood by for defensive patrols. In the absence of any night fighters, a pair of Fairey Gordons was borrowed for night patrols until, eventually, No. 29 was recalled to the U.K.

Arriving at Southampton on 12 September, 1936 the squadron was soon re-established at North Weald where, a year later, it received Demons fitted with open gun-turrets to assist the gunners in traversing their guns in the slipstream. In November 1937, a move to the new airfield at Debden (Essex) was made and, in December 1938, the Demons were replaced by more modern aircraft—the two-motor Bristol Blenheim.

The twin-engined Bristol Type 142 light-transport had demonstrated a remarkable performance when test-flown and a military version (the Type 142M) was ordered. This became the Bristol Blenheim light-bomber which out-flew most of the fighters in service when it first reached the R.A.F. As an interim measure, some Blenheims were supplied to fighter squadrons and, since they already had trained gunners, the Demon squadrons were selected. A forward-firing four-gun tray of 0.303-in Brownings was fixed under the fuselage to provide the main armament and No. 29's crews began adapting to two engines, retractable undercarriages, gun turrets and enclosed cockpits.

By the outbreak of the Second World War it was already evident that the Blenheim fighter could be no match for the new single-seat monoplanes so that their use was envisaged as night fighters. In December 1939, mysterious pieces of equipment were being fitted to a few Blenheims but it was the summer of 1940 before this became normal as aircraft interception (A.I.) radar left the experimental stage. Most night patrols relied on searchlights or ground radar stations to guide them towards a suspected enemy and from that point all interceptions had to be visual. The multiplicity of glazed panels in the nose of the Blenheim presented pilots with a panorama of reflecting instrument lights through which the dark shapes of night bombers had to be located.

Little success was met until 18 June 1940 when Pilot Officer J. D. Humphreys and Sergeant E. H. Bee in L1375 located a Heinkel He 111 lit by searchlights near Bury St. Edmunds. Closing in from below, fire was opened at 100-feet range with the front guns and the enemy's port engine began to smoke. Return fire hit the starboard petrol tank of the Blenheim and also put the hydraulics out of action. This forced the British fighter to retire while the enemy made-off on fire. Half-an-hour later, a Blenheim was seen attacking another Heinkel which went down in flames but Pilot Officer J. S. Barnwell and his gunner Sergeant Long in L6636 did not return to base and were presumed to have crashed in the sea after this action.

As radar operators became more accustomed to their cranky radar sets, more enemy bombers were found but many futile pursuits took place during which the radar lost contact or went out of action. Three He 111s were claimed destroyed during August but night patrols were responsible for several accidents.

On 2 September 1940, a Bristol Beaufighter (R2072) arrived as a first step in re-equipping the squadron with an effective night-fighter. Beaufighter R2072 was surrounded by an admiring throng which noted the heavy armament (four 20-mm cannon in the nose and six 0.303-in machine guns in the wings) the large flat bulletproof windscreen offering an excellent field of view and the pair of powerful Bristol Hercules radial engines which gave it a top speed of 320 m.p.h. There was no provision for gunners but the radar operator had a cockpit aft fitted with a Perspex blister giving an excellent all-round view. On the night of 17 September the first Beaufighter sortie was flown but it was not until February 1941 that sufficient Beaufighters were on strength to replace the Blenheims.

One of the pilots who arrived in November 1940 was Flight Lieutenant Guy Gibson, later to become famous as the leader of the 'Dambusters' of No. 617 Squadron and destined to win the Victoria Cross.

A Beaufighter (R2095) was lost on 17 November when its port engine failed. Squadron Leader S. C. Widdows, No. 29's Commanding Officer, found the aircraft out of control and ordered his observer, Pilot Officer L. D. Wilson, to abandon ship. Wilson was unable to open his escape hatch and Widdows, who had started to get out of the awkward pilot's hatch, realised he was trapped. He climbed back into his seat and managed to make a belly-landing at Walker's Farm near Sleaford (Lincolnshire) where, fortunately, R2095 did not catch fire. Wilson was released with nothing worse than broken ankles.

As German bombers attacked cities throughout the British Isles, encounters were more frequent. On the night of 13/14 March, the seaport of Liverpool was the target and enemy bombers were crossing the East Coast on their way to and from their objective. Flying Officer Bob Braham and Sergeant Ross (in R2144) found a Dornier Do 17 off the Norfolk coast which blew up after a burst of fire from 60 yards. Later the Commanding Officer, now a Wing Commander, with Sergeant Ryall as radar operator crept up on a Ju 88 over Lincolnshire. A short burst by Wing Commander Widdows at 100 yards range sent it into the ground near Horncastle. The following evening Gibson (in R2094) with Sergeant James attacked an He 111 but had his cannon jam. The observer in a Beaufighter had access to the breeches from his cockpit and rectified the fault but after another short burst they stopped firing again. Parts of the enemy bomber dented the Beaufighter's wings as it crashed two miles off Skegness (Lincolnshire).

Next month, the squadron moved south to West Malling (Kent) where the direct route for bombing London resulted in many more interceptions and the toll of enemy bombers grew. By midsummer night raiding had decreased considerably as enemy bomber units were transferred to the Russian Front. During the following winter, a greater proportion of German bombers crossing the coast was destroyed as improved radar equipment and techniques made interception

1

2

3

1 Squadron Siskins lined up at Hendon for the 1929 Display; some carry camera guns on the top wing. (*Photo: Ministry of Defence H.15, I.W.M. Q.69699.*)

2 No. 29 Squadron Siskins in formation. (*Photo: I.W.M. Q.69700.*)

3 Bulldog K2210 fitted with a camera gun on the top wing. In place of the three crosses carried on Siskins, Bulldogs were marked with one each side of the roundel. (*Photo: Ministry of Defence H.2216.*)

1

1 Armstrong Whitworth Siskin IIIA J8664 was one of the first batch of these fighters received by No. 29 Squadron in March 1928.

2 D.H.2 No. 7846 carried no individual marking to indicate No. 29 Squadron and was destroyed in a crash on Le Hameau airfield on 28 November 1916.

3 Hawker Demon K3976 was delivered to No. 29 Squadron in March 1935 and was taken to the Middle East. Brought back to England in September 1936 it was passed to No. 25 Squadron in January 1938 and became a ground instruction airframe (serial 1405M) in April 1939.

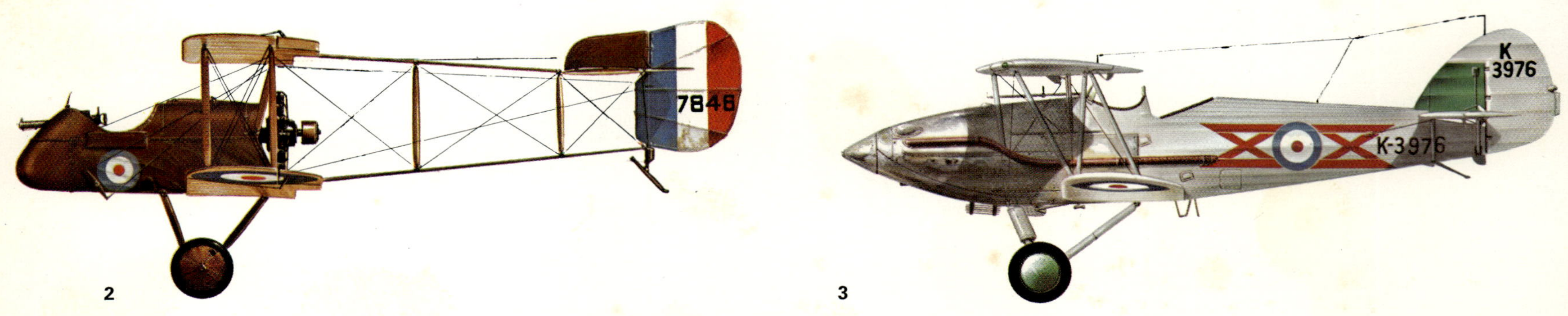

2

3

1

1 Armstrong Whitworth Meteor NF.11 WD602 served with No. 29 Squadron between August 1951 and September 1954. It was later transferred to the Belgian Air Force.

2 Bristol Beaufighter IF V8324 served with No. 29 Squadron between July and November 1942 and was named 'Bambi'.

3 De Havilland Mosquito NF.36 RL210 was built in August 1945 and joined No. 29 Squadron in November 1949. It was written-off in a belly-landing on 1 February 1950, ending up in a hedge.

2

3

1-2

3-4

5-6

1 'B-for-Bambi', a Beaufighter I of No. 29 Squadron, carried an individual emblem on its nose. Such decoration was very unusual on night fighters. V8324 served with the squadron from July to November, 1942. (*Photo: I.W.M. CH.7741.*)

2 Javelin FAW.6 XH700 at Leuchars in June 1959 shows the unusual crew entry ladder designed for Javelins. (*Photo: Leuchars 3100.*)

3 Mosquito XIII HK382 at Hunsdon in January 1945 carries long-range tanks for use on intruder missions. (*Photo: No. 29 Squadron collection.*)

4 Javelin FAW.9s with four long-range tanks at N'dola, Zambia in 1966. (*Photo: Times of Zambia.*)

5 No. 29 Squadron parades at the end of its Javelin period on the apron at Wattisham. (*Photo: No. 29 Squadron collection.*)

6 Resembling mediaeval lances more than instruments of air power, the refuelling probes of No. 29 Squadron Javelins permitted lengthy deployments with the help of tanker aircraft. (*Photo: Akrotiri A.2137.*)

easier. On 31 October 1942, Flying Officer G. Pepper and Pilot Officer J. H. Toone in Beaufighter V8233 took off at 18:20 to patrol over Kent. Near Canterbury a blip on the radar screen turned into a Dornier Do 217. After two bursts the bomber's starboard engine caught fire and it dived away. The Beaufighter overshot and turned to see the Dornier still flying so fired another long burst from 500 feet and the enemy fell into the sea off Dungeness.

Returning to refuel, Pepper and Toone were airborne again at 23:25 and obtained another contact in the same area as before. The target opened fire and after a 3-second burst from the Beaufighter went into a spin, its bombload exploding as it hit the ground. Ground control vectored the Beaufighter on to yet another Do 217 which dived into the sea after receiving two burst of cannon fire. A fourth Do 217 was destroyed by Braham off Broadstairs on the same night.

Another memorable night for No. 29 Squadron was that of 17/18 January 1943, when up to 50 enemy aircraft attacked London. The squadron flew 27 sorties during the raid and the first contact was by Flight Sergeant Wood—of the Royal Australian Air Force—and Pilot Officer Slaughter (in V7579) when they used up all their ammunition on a Ju 88 without seeing it crash. Flying Officer A. C. Musgrove and Sergeant J. Petrie (in X7845) attacked a Ju 88 which was last seen diving in flames. At this time the C.O., Wing Commander C. M. Wight-Boycott, flying with Flying Officer E. A. Sanders (in V8270) was diverted from an exercise with ground control to intercept a Do 217. The Beaufighter opened fire and the enemy bomber dived vertically towards the sea off Folkestone. Another blip appeared on the screen and enabled a few short bursts to be fired in the direction of a spiralling bomber.

After refuelling the same crew took off again and this time a Do 217 went down in flames near Westerham (Kent). Immediately a second was spotted which began violent evasive action. A chase developed in which two bursts hit the enemy bomber which caught fire and spun away. At this point the pilot was feeling ill and found that his oxygen had been accidentally turned off. He recovered in time to see a Ju 88 over Caterham (Surrey) and attack it. The bomber caught fire and the crew of four baled out.

Having ended his period of command in style, Wight-Boycott handed over to Wing Commander C. M. Miller. He, in turn, while flying V8282 30 miles east of Foulness (Essex) was vectored on to a German mine-layer by Squadron Leader Mawhood at Foreness control. The radar operator, Flight Lieutenant J. P. Crowther made a contact at three miles which turned out to be a Do 217 at 700 feet. Creeping up some 200 feet below the Dornier, the bomber's mission was confirmed by two parachute mines narrowly missing the Beaufighter on their way to the sea. At 150 yards range, fire was opened and the Dornier dived into the sea. A second Do 217 was on the controller's screen and Miller was vectored on to it. After attacking from 150 yards the Dornier pulled up, a collision was narrowly avoided before the mine-layer went into the sea.

Intruder missions over France began on 16 April 1943, when Pilot Officers Cronie and Colebrook took X7679 on a tour of the Pas de Calais which ended by shooting up a barge on the Seine. On the same night, a pair of Focke-Wulf FW 190s landed at West Malling under the impression they were home safely. Losses among conventional bombers had forced the Germans to use fast single-seat fighters as night bombers though their pilots' preoccupation with navigation resulted in many being surprised and destroyed by the slower night fighters.

In May 1943, de Havilland Mosquitos began to arrive and the Beaufighters ended their service with the squadron by accounting for the 50th enemy aircraft to be destroyed at night. On 20 May, Pilot Officers Crone and Colebrook took X7679 to Dijon where they found Longvic airfield illuminated. An aircraft displaying navigation lights approached from the south and they closed, firing two bursts at an He 111 which spiralled into the ground and blew up 10 miles south of the airfield.

Initially, the A.I. Mark VIII radar in the new Mosquito XIIs could not be taken over enemy territory so it was not until May 1944 that the squadron was permitted to use its Mosquitos with this mark of radar—the first centrimetric, spinning-dish scanner—over enemy territory. A few Mosquito VIs allotted were taken away before use but once permission was given the Mosquito XIIIs (heavier, longer-range Mk. XIIs) ranged over Northern France, the Low Countries and Germany attacking communications and seeking out enemy aircraft. In February 1945, the squadron moved to Colerne (Wiltshire) to convert to Mosquito 30s and took them to Manston (Kent) early in April. Few operations were flown before the end of the war and No. 29 returned to West Malling (also in Kent) in October to form part of the post-war fighter defences. In one of the last operational flights, Warrant Officer Dallinson shot down a Messerschmitt Me 262 jet fighter and damaged a second in the squadron's first encounter with the future generation of fighter aircraft.

All-weather Fighters

No. 29 Squadron did not, as so many squadrons did, disband after the end of the war. It continued to fly Mosquito night-fighters for six years over Southern England before receiving its first jet fighters. In August 1951, Armstrong Whitworth-built Gloster Meteor NF.11s, a two-seat variant of the Meteor single-seat day-fighter, reached the squadron and improved vastly its chances of making successful interceptions at night.

Eventually, to replace the Meteor and Vampire night-fighters a new type was developed in the early 1950s. The Gloster Javelin was a large delta-winged fighter powered by a pair of Sapphire engines. Radar was housed in a large pointed radome in the nose and four 30-mm Aden guns carried in the wings. The fighter (all-weather) Javelin FAW.6s which re-equipped No. 29 in November 1957 had a top speed of 600 m.p.h. at 50,000 feet, greatly increasing the effectiveness of the air defences.

In 1961, the Mark 6s were replaced by Mark 9s armed with Firestreak missiles. In the interests of mobility, a large refuelling probe was fitted to permit air refuelling from Vickers Valiant and, later, Handley Page Victor tankers.

The squadron left Britain for the first time since 1936 when it flew out to Cyprus in February, 1963. After nearly three years it was on the move again, this time to Zambia in one of the oddest deployments ever experienced by the R.A.F.

Alarmed by the decision of Rhodesia to declare its independence, neighbouring Zambia asked for support from Britain to counter the efficient Royal Rhodesian Air Force and was rewarded with a squadron of Javelins from Cyprus. No. 29 Squadron arrived at Ndola civil airport early in December 1965 and remained based there for 9 months.

There was an air of complete unreality about the whole episode. The "enemy" consisted almost entirely of former R.A.F. personnel who would have given short shrift to anyone displaying hostility to the Javelins. Rhodesian navigational and meteorological services were available and No. 29's sole casualty was XH890 which folded up its undercarriage while landing at Ndola on 2 June, 1966 and was picked clean by the engineering section seeking spares for the other Javelins. It was with some relief that the squadron made its way back to Cyprus at the end of August.

No. 29's stay in the Mediterranean was to be short. In May 1967, the Javelins were flown back to Britain and the squadron was re-equipped with English Electric Lightnings, shedding its navigators after many years of teamwork. With the Javelin, the night-fighter had become the all-weather fighter and the Lightning represented the ultimate in this role. With a top speed of around Mach 2.2 (about 1,500 m.p.h. at 40,000 feet) the missile-armed fighters joined No. 111 Squadron at Wattisham (Suffolk) as part of the fighter defences of the United Kingdom, a far cry from the chattering D.H.2s No. 29 first went to war in.

SQUADRON BASES

Gosport, Hampshire	7 November 1915
St. Omer, France	25 March 1916
Abeele, France	15 April 1916
Le Hameau, France	23 October 1916
Poperinghe, Belgium	5 July 1917
La Lovie, France	16 February 1918
Teteghem, France	11 April 1918
St. Omer, France	22 April 1918
Vignacourt, France	11 June 1918
St. Omer, France	22 July 1918
Hoog Huis, France	1 August 1918
La Lovie, France	25 September 1918
Hoog Huis, France	5 October 1918
Marcke, Belgium	23 October 1918
Nivelles, Belgium	26 November 1918
Bickendorf, Germany	19 December 1918
Spittlegate, Lincolnshire	10 August 1919 to 31 December 1919
Duxford, Cambridgeshire	1 April 1923
North Weald, Essex	1 April 1928
Embarked for Egypt	4 October 1935
Amriya, Egypt	31 October 1935
Helwan, Egypt	20 July 1936
Aboukir, Egypt	6 August 1936
North Weald, Essex	12 September 1936
Debden, Essex	22 November 1937
Drem, East Lothian	4 April 1940
Debden, Essex	10 May 1940
Digby, Lincolnshire	June 1940
Wellingore, Lincolnshire	8 July 1940
West Malling, Kent	27 April 1941
Bradwell Bay, Essex	13 May 1943
Ford, Sussex	3 September 1943
Drem, East Lothian	29 February 1944
West Malling, Kent	1 May 1944
Hunsdon, Hertfordshire	19 June 1944
Colerne, Wiltshire	22 February 1945
Manston, Kent	11 May 1945
West Malling, Kent	29 October 1945
Tangmere, Sussex	30 November 1950
Acklington, Northumberland	14 January 1957
Leuchars, Fifeshire	22 July 1958
Nicosia, Cyprus	28 February 1963
Akrotiri, Cyprus	16 March 1964
Ndola, Zambia	3 December 1965
Akrotiri, Cyprus	1 September 1966
Wattisham, Suffolk	10 May 1967

SQUADRON EQUIPMENT
Period of Use & Typical Serial and Code Letters

Aircraft	Period of Use	Serial and Code
Maurice Farman	November 1915 to March 1916	2947
Avro 504A	November 1915 to March 1916	4768
Caudron G.III	November 1915 to March 1916	
B.E.2c	December 1915 to March 1916	2065
B.E.2b	February 1916 to March 1916	2886
D.H.2	March 1916 to March 1917	A2551
F.E.8	June 1916 to August 1916	6381
Nieuport 17, (& 27)	March 1917 to April 1918	B1605
S.E.5a	April 1918 to August 1919	F899 (C)
Sopwith Snipe	April 1924 to January 1925	
Gloucestershire (Gloster) Grebe II	January 1925 to March 1928	J7390
Armstrong Whitworth Siskin IIIA	March 1928 to June 1932	J9912
Bristol Bulldog IIA	June 1932 to April 1935	K2866
Hawker Demon	March 1935 to August 1936	K3774
	October 1936 to December 1938	K5898
Fairey Gordon	March 1936 to August 1936	
Bristol Blenheim IF	December 1938 to February 1941	K7135 (RO-L)
Hawker Hurricane I	August 1940 to December 1940	P3201
Bristol Beaufighter I	November 1940 to June 1943	R2138 (RO-L)
Bristol Beaufighter VI	March 1943 to May 1943	EL165
de Havilland Mosquito XII	May 1943 to April 1944	HK129 (RO-G)
de Havilland Mosquito XIII	October 1943 to February 1945	HK522 (RO-L)
de Havilland Mosquito VI	July 1943 to August 1943	HP852
de Havilland Mosquito 30	February 1945 to August 1946	NT417 (RO-E)
	October 1950 to August 1951	RK937
de Havilland Mosquito NF.36	August 1946 to October 1950	RL175 (RO-P)
Gloster Meteor NF.11	August 1951 to November 1957	WD722 (E)
Gloster Meteor NF.12	February 1958 to July 1958	WS593
Gloster Javelin FAW.6	November 1957 to May 1961	XA825 (K)
Gloster Javelin FAW.9	April 1961 to May 1967	XH848 (L)
English Electric Lightning F.3	May 1967 to date	XR718 (C)

COMMANDING OFFICERS

Major L.Daws	7 November 1915
Major E.L.Conran MC	25 May 1916
Major W.A.Gratton-Bellew MC	5 September 1916
Major H.V.C.de Crespigny MC	22 March 1917
Major C.M.B.Chapman MC	21 July 1917
Major H.V.C.de Crespigny MC	4 October 1917
Major C.H.Dixon	20 November 1917
Major H.E.White	9 February 1919
S/Ldr. The Hon.L.J.E. Twistleton-Wykeham-Fiennes	1 April 1923
S/Ldr. R.H.G.Neville MC	12 August 1924
S/Ldr. M.L.Taylor AFC	10 August 1927
S/Ldr. P.G.E.Scott	6 December 1929
S/Ldr. E.J.D.Routh	9 June 1930
S/Ldr. H.D.O' Neill AFC	14 April 1931
S/Ldr. J.H.Butler	18 August 1933
S/Ldr. C.Chapman DSC	20 August 1934
S/Ldr. E.P.Mackay	10 December 1935
S/Ldr. D.M.Fleming	14 April 1936
S/Ldr. J.B.Lynch	19 August 1936
S/Ldr. R.C.Jonas	17 December 1937
S/Ldr. M.W.S.Robinson	2 December 1938
S/Ldr. P.S.Gomez	13 February 1939
S/Ldr. E.R.Bitmead	8 July 1940
S/Ldr. S.C.Widdows DFC	16 July 1940
W/Cdr. E.L.Colbeck-Welch DFC	13 June 1941
W/Cdr. R.Cleland	10 July 1942
W/Cdr. C.M.Wight-Boycott DSO	10 September 1942
W/Cdr. C.M.Miller DFC	29 January 1943
W/Cdr. R.E.X.Mack DFC	12 June 1943
S/Ldr. P.W.Arbon DFC	23 February 1944
W/Cdr. G.F.Powell-Sheddon DFC	29 April 1944
W/Cdr. J.W.Allan DSO, DFC	18 December 1944
S/Ldr. T.C.Wood DFC	31 December 1945
S/Ldr. D.Hawkins DFC	1 November 1946
S/Ldr. M.J.B.Young DFC	10 March 1949
S/Ldr. M.Shaw DSO	7 July 1949
S/Ldr. H.E.Bodien DSO, DFC	15 August 1951
S/Ldr. B.P.T.Horsley AFC	30 June 1952
S/Ldr. E.B.Sismore DSO, DFC	11 May 1953
W/Cdr. J.A.C.Aiken	2 January 1956
W/Cdr. W.Harbison AFC	2 January 1958
W/Cdr. A.R.Gordon-Cumming	15 July 1959
W/Cdr. R.E.Gardiner DFC	3 July 1961
W/Cdr. E.G.P.Jeffery	18 April 1962
W/Cdr. K.Burge	1 January 1965
W/Cdr. R.Neil	23 November 1966
S/Ldr. L.A.Boyer	10 May 1967
W/Cdr. L.W.Phipps AFC	18 September 1967
W/Cdr. B.Carroll	20 October 1969

No.54 Squadron

A formation of No. 54 Squadron Bulldogs over Plymouth while on fighter affiliation exercises with the flying boat squadrons at Mount Batten. (*Photo: Flight International 14800.*)

The Opening Round

By the time No. 54 Squadron was formed on 15 May 1916, air fighting had become an established factor in air warfare. From improvisation using standard reconnaissance aircraft, specialized fighters had been developed and No. 54 was fortunate in being the recipients of the first Sopwith Pups to go into service with the Royal Flying Corps.

Before these were delivered, the squadron had been training at Castle Bromwich near Birmingham with B.E.2cs and the ubiquitous Avro 504s. Apart from training, No. 54 was also given the task of providing defensive aircraft in the event of enemy Zeppelins attacking Birmingham though none was ever sighted. In September, Pups began to be delivered from the Sopwith works at Kingston-on-Thames (Surrey) and the squadron began to re-equip.

The Pup was a small biplane powered by a 80 h.p. Le Rhone rotary which gave it a top speed of 111 m.p.h. at ground level. It had excellent handling qualities which, combined with the fixed-mounted but synchronized Vickers machine-gun, made the Pup a potent fighter. From October onwards, pilots practised on their new mounts until the day came in December when the journey to France began. Staging through

London Colney (Hertfordshire) and St. Omer, the squadron reached its base at Bertangles on 26 December 1916.

At first, the Pups were restricted by the urgent necessity of providing day bombers with escorts. Naval Pups (Royal Naval Air Service) from Dunkirk had proved to the Germans how effective a fighter the type was and enemy fighters tended to avoid tangling with Pup formations. As a result, while the main purpose was attained in that the bombers were relatively unhampered by enemy fighters, No. 54 seldom had a chance to engage in dogfights for which the Pups were so suited. It was April before the first enemy aircraft, an Albatros D.III, was shot down by Captain W. V. Strugnall. Enemy observation balloons were also targets for the nimble fighters during the Battle of Arras. After Arras, No. 54 was moved to the Flanders coast.

Such was the rapid development of aircraft at this time that what had been regarded as a superlative fighter nine months earlier now became obsolescent. To augment the single machine-gun, some aircraft were fitted with a Lewis gun on the top wing but this was found to be unsatisfactory as the weight tended to weaken the lightly-built wing centre-section. For ground-attack work, bomb racks were fitted to enable 20-lb Cooper bombs to be carried but bomb-carrying was unpopular because they detracted from the performance. It was time for the Pup to be replaced by something more powerful.

The new aircraft received during the first half of December 1917 were Sopwith Camels. They resembled the Pups in design but had an armament of two fixed, forward-firing Vickers guns. It was slightly slower than the Pup in its original form and its flying characteristics shocked pilots used to tractability of the Pup. It was highly manoeuvrable and probably the best 'dogfighting' aircraft of the war, but it was also a potential killer of inexperienced or careless pilots. Because of the closely-grouped mass of engine, guns and pilot, it could turn very tightly; too tightly on occasions when over-reaction caused the aircraft to spin quickly without any warning. The all-too-brief conversion courses were insufficient to train pilots adequately and there were many accidents. But once the Camel had been mastered it was the equal of any enemy fighter.

The massive German offensive in March 1918 resulted in many fighter squadrons being diverted to ground-attack duties. With little space left between the advancing Germans and the Channel ports on which the Army depended, an all-out effort was made to stop the onrush. No. 54's Camels spent most of their time machine-gunning enemy troops and supply columns. A captured report on one attack by the squadron

1

2

demonstrated how low these attacks took place. During an attack on a company of troops, the company commander escaped being hit by throwing himself flat only to be run over by a Camel's wheels. As was to be expected, small-arms fire accounted for many aircraft and it was seldom that any Camel was free from fabric patches over bullet holes. Twenty-pounder Cooper bombs were carried in racks under the wings throughout the last eight months of the war.

By the time the German army was in full retreat, No. 54 was one of many squadrons harrying the survivors. German fighters were still to be seen and were being strafed on their airfields to clear the way for the R.A.F. day-bombers formations. On 4 November 1918, 17 Camels dropped 66 bombs on an enemy airfield near Leuze and machine-gunned the buildings. Two hangars were set on fire and two others hit. Six Fokker D.VIIs appeared and Captain G. H. Hackwill engaged them, only to have his guns jam and see the enemy escape into clouds. Lieutenant J. C. MacLennan (in F2083) found a German two-seater in a field with mechanics working on it and fired 350 rounds into it. He was then attacked by four D.VIIs which disappeared when a Sopwith Snipe came to his aid.

On the day before the Armistice, 16 Camels from the squadron dropped 57 twenty-five-pounders on the battered railway station at Enghien. The rails leading north-west were blocked and several freight wagons wrecked. The fighters then went on to machine-gun road vehicles and three aircraft sighted on an airfield near Croisette. In the afternoon, 17 aircraft repeated the operation. It was the last major attack before the war ended. At 10:45 on 11 November, Lieutenant A. T. Holman (in F2148) took off on a low-flying sortie; fifteen minutes later, the First World War ended.

The war had cost the squadron 44 pilots killed and 25 taken prisoner. On 22 January 1919, No. 54 handed over its Camels to No. 151 Squadron and next month returned to the U.K. where it remained as a cadre until disbanded on 25 October, 1919.

Home Defence

During the 1920s, the defences of the United Kingdom included only a small number of fighter squadrons. More had been authorized but in the financial climate of the times these took a long time to appear. One squadron for the defence of London was to be based at Hornchurch in Essex and on 15 January 1930 it was formed as No. 54 (Fighter) Squadron.

Aircraft for the new squadron were in short supply and to bridge the gap between the formation of the unit and the delivery of Bristol Bulldogs, No. 54 was restricted to forming a headquarters and one flight of dual-control Armstrong Whitworth Siskins. These

3

1 No. 54 Squadron pilots pose before one of the squadron's Camels soon after the end of World War One. A variety of styles of cold-weather flying clothing is in use. (*Photo: I.W.M. Q.11859.*)

2 Bulldogs ready for take-off at Hornchurch. K1641 nearest the camera is fitted with a camera gun. (*Photo: Ministry of Defence H.752.*)

3 The remains of one of a section of three Spitfire Is caught by German bombs in the act of taking off from Hornchurch on 31 August 1940. (*Photo: Ministry of Defence H.2038.*)

conversions of the Siskin fighter were to remain in service until October 1930. The squadron's first Bulldog arrived on 8 April followed by two more at intervals but one was lost on 29 April when Pilot Officer T. B. Byrne's aircraft broke up in a 'bunt'* and he abandoned it in haste. When the squadron left for its first armament course at Sutton Bridge (Lincolnshire) at the end of July it had only four Bulldogs on strength; it was October before it was fully equipped.

Training in day and night fighter tactics occupied the squadron for year after year. Restricted by the performance of biplane fighters, the air defence system improved only slowly; the revolution to be brought about by the adoption of radar still lay in the future. So, in overcast weather or darkness, fighters had to depend on Army-manned sound detectors of dubious effectiveness reporting the enemy's position which was then passed by radio from ground control rooms.

Conversion to Gloster Gauntlets in September 1936 raised the top speed of No. 54's fighters by nearly 60 m.p.h. but the armament remained at two 0.303-in. machine-guns. At the same time, permission was obtained to change the squadrons' coloured markings to red bars, the original yellow scheme being judged as inappropriate for fighters.

Expansion of the Royal Air Force was under way and on 15 March 1937, 'B' Flight was detached to form the basis of No. 87 Squadron reforming at Tangmere. Improved-performance Gloster Gladiators replaced the Gauntlets in May and in October were inspected by the future enemy in the shape of *Luftwaffe* Generals Milch, Stumpff and Udet on a courtesy visit!

The defensive radar network was beginning to take shape and in March 1938 the old Vickers machine-guns in the Gladiators were replaced by new Brownings of much greater reliability and increased rate-of-fire.

Effectiveness increased immeasurably in March 1939 when the squadron received its first Supermarine Spitfire. The Gladiators were transferred to No. 603 (City of Edinburgh) Squadron, Auxiliary Air Force to convert yet another auxiliary squadron from day bombers to fighters. On the outbreak of war on 3 September 1939, the squadron had 16 Spitfires plus five in reserve.

One of the first tasks was to add armour to the aircraft. A multiple-layer windscreen replaced the original Triplex screen, armour plate fitted to the engine bulkhead and a heavy duralumin deflector shield provided over the top fuselage tank forward of the cockpit. The emphasis on forward-facing protection indicated the anti-bomber role foreseen for Spitfires. From December, aircraft with Rotol propellers began to reach the squadron and enhanced the performance of the Spitfire.

Few enemy aircraft came near the Hornchurch (Essex) sector until the invasion of the Low Countries in May 1940. No. 54 began operating over the Belgian coast on 16 May with a morning patrol by 12 Spitfires over Ostend without incident, repeated during the afternoon with similar results. Patrols continued daily and, on 21 May, Flight Lieutenant J. A. Leathart damaged a Heinkel He 111. On the same day, Pilot Officer J. L. Allen was sent off in Spitfire N3188 on a lone sortie to identify a doubtful aircraft spotted on radar. Radar (then known as radio-location) was not always capable at its current state of development of identifying the size of formations as Allen found when he came upon 30 Junkers Ju 88s near the Belgian coast. Overtaking a straggler, he opened fire at 150 yards range and both engines of the bomber began to smoke. It vanished into the huge smoke pall over Dunkirk.

Next day, Leathart left Hornchurch in the squadron's Miles Master advanced trainer (N7681) to collect Squadron Leader White of No. 74 Squadron who had force-landed on Calais aerodrome. With it as escort went Pilot Officers A. C. 'Al' Deere and J. L. Allen in Spitfires N3180 and P9389. It was fortunate that they did for, after picking up White, Flight Lieutenant Leathart began his take-off as several Messerschmitt Bf 109s dived on the airfield. The two Spitfires spotted the enemy and engaged them as the Master weaved back to the airfield. One Bf 109 hit the ground while Leathart was on approach and a second hit the ground in flames as he touched down. A third fell into the sea a few miles from Calais. Having expended all their ammunition, the Spitfires headed for home leaving Leathart to wait until the skies became safer for unarmed trainers—even Rolls-Royce Kestrel-powered Masters. In No. 54's first engagement with enemy fighters the squadron was encouraged to discover that their Spitfires with Rotol propellers were faster than the Messerschmitts.

Two days later, Leathart led the squadron on patrol over the Dunkirk beaches when two large formations of Heinkel He 111s were sighted. A formation attack on the bombers was foiled by the escorting Messerschmitts and the action became a series of individual battles. All the Spitfires returned to lodge claims for nine enemy fighters destroyed. Four hours later the squadron was back for the third time that day. A dozen Bf 109s were engaged and four destroyed. Two Spitfires force-landed on the beach between Dunkirk and Calais and their pilots, Flying Officer Linley and Sergeant Phillips, were seen standing nearby. Later both aircraft (P9455 and P9388) were observed from the air to be burnt out presumably destroyed to prevent them falling into enemy hands.

On 25 May, the squadron escorted 11 Fleet Air Arm Fairey Swordfish biplanes on a bombing raid to the Gravelines-Calais area. The elderly three-seaters proceeding at a stately 90 knots to bomb the enemy in broad daylight underlined the seriousness of the position as German divisions rolled across Flanders to the Channel ports. The Spitfires kept a large number of Bf 109s and Bf 110s away from the Fleet Air Arm torpedo-bombers and claimed the destruction of two Bf 109s and three Bf 110s. Pilot Officer Allen's N3188 was hit in the engine and while gliding down caught fire. The pilot baled-out and was picked up by British destroyers. Pilot Officer George Gribble in N3103 force-landed on the Dunkirk beaches and joined the evacuation while Sergeant Buckland was missing in N3096.

Patrols were continuous until 28 May, the Spitfires refuelling and rearming between missions in the short periods when they were on the ground. Seven German aircraft were claimed on 26 May and two more on 27 May when Flight Lieutenant Pearson went missing in N3030. On 28 May, the squadron was out early and attacked a Dornier Do 17 which escaped into cloud. 'Al' Deere's Spitfire (N3180) was hit in the engine and force-landed in Belgium; the pilot returning home in a destroyer. On this day, No. 54 was ordered to Catterick (Yorkshire) to rest. In 10 days of intensive operations it had claimed 31 enemy aircraft destroyed for the loss of four pilots and seven Spitfires. Leathart was awarded the Distinguished Service Order, Deere and Allen received the Distinguished Flying Cross and Sergeant Phillips gained the Distinguished Flying Medal, for their part in the actions over Dunkirk.

The rest period did not last long. On 4 June, the squadron returned to Hornchurch to fly defensive patrols over the Thames Estuary and once, on 17 June, to patrol over Abbeville as the last remnants of a defensive line crumbled. Few enemy aircraft were met but a foretaste of the future came on 4 July when two aircraft were surprised and damaged by low-flying Bf 109s near Manston. Three days later Green Section of 'B' Flight attacked an He 111 in the same area and were, in turn, 'jumped' by fighters. Two of the three Spitfires were damaged and one force-landed near Deal.

Next day, the squadron intercepted some Bf 109s between Deal and Dover and claimed two destroyed. These were later confirmed as one from *Lehrgeschwader 2* (*L.G.2*—an operational training *Geschwader*) and one from *Jagdgeschwader 51* (*J.G.51*).

On 9 July, 'A' Flight was patrolling over the Channel when they met an unexpected sight. A large

* 'Bunt': A vertically induced half-loop resulting in inverted flight attitude—Editor.

white two-motor biplane with huge twin floats was flying at a leisurely pace over the Goodwin Sands. After an attack by Pilot Officer J. L. Allen the seaplane, a Heinkel He 59 of *Seenotflugkommando 1*, landed on the Goodwin Sands whence it was towed to Deal by the Walmer lifeboat. The crew became prisoners.

While this was taking place, the remainder of the squadron was engaged with the escort of Bf 109s from *J.G.51*. 'Al' Deere's N3183 was damaged in a head-on collision with a Messerschmitt which hit the Spitfire's cockpit canopy and propeller. The engine stopped and he glided back to Manston. The aircraft caught fire on landing but Deere escaped with slight burns. Pilot Officers J. W. Garton (R6705) and A. Evershed (L1093) were both shot down and killed but one Bf 109 was confirmed as crashed in the sea off Dover.

Until 26 July, when the squadron returned to Catterick, No. 54 was engaged in covering convoys passing through the Straits of Dover. When the 12 Spitfires flew off to the north, only six of the pilots serving with the squadron before Dunkirk were still on strength.

Returning to Hornchurch on 8 August, the squadron was back in action during one of the most vital periods of the Battle of Britain. On 12 August, large numbers of Messerschmitts covering an attack on Manston were found over Kent. Three were shot down, two from *J.G.3* and one from *J.G.26*, while a fourth was claimed but not confirmed. Two Spitfires force-landed and were written-off but later in the day a Bf 110 of *Erprobungsgruppe 210* was destroyed over Manston and the crew captured.

15 August was the day when the *Luftwaffe* made a supreme effort to eliminate the British fighter force as a prelude to invasion. Eighty German aircraft were lost, all but four in combat, while 28 R.A.F. fighters were shot down or damaged beyond immediate repair. A force of Junkers Ju 87 dive-bombers, escorted by Bf 109s, carried out an attack on Hawkinge (Kent) airfield but was intercepted by 12 Spitfires of 54 Squadron and 11 Hawker Hurricanes of 501 Squadron. Sergeant N. A. Lawrence flying Spitfire N3097 succeeded in destroying three of the *Stukas* before being shot down in the sea by the escort. The three Ju 87s were confirmed and Lawrence was picked up by the Royal Navy. Sergeant W. Klosinski, the first of No. 54's Polish pilots, was forced down near Ashford (Kent) in R7015 and injured. But Hawkinge was saved from major damage by the timely intervention of the two fighter squadrons. In the early evening 'Al' Deere was forced to abandon R6981 when it was hit over Kent but escaped with a sprained ankle on landing.

Spitfire VCs of No. 54 Squadron over Darwin. Desert filters are fitted and the camouflage of 'K', dark green and dark earth differs from the desert scheme on the other two. (*Photo: No. 54 Squadron archives.*)

During the next two weeks, patrols were being flown at high intensity. The fighter squadrons were fully extended and almost always outnumbered because of the short warning time available to carry out a fast climb to get above the approaching enemy. Inevitably, it always appeared that the Bf 109s were high above when the Spitfires and Hurricanes reached the scene.

On 26 August, Leathart was transferred from the squadron to the Air Ministry for a well-earned rest from operational flying. To take his place came Squadron Leader Donald Finlay—a noted Olympics athlete—who had served with No. 54 in 1937. His stay on this occasion was short as next day he was shot down in X4058 and injured while Deere was once more shot down and baled out safely. This time, a Spitfire pilot with acute recognition trouble was thought to be responsible.

The final blow came on 31 August when a force of enemy bombers approached Hornchurch. The squadron 'scrambled' 11 aircraft and eight of these had just left the ground when the first of about 60 bombs began to carpet the airfield. The last three Spitfires were just becoming airborne when bombs burst around them. Pilot Officer E. F. Edsall crash-landed and climbed out in time to rescue 'Al' Deere. The latter's Spitfire had one wing blown off and had slewed upside down across the airfield. The third member of the section, Sergeant J. Davis, was blown into a field across the stream bordering Hornchurch and walked back, finding some difficulty in gaining access to his home station again. How all three pilots survived the complete destruction of their aircraft is impossible to say. Five of the attacking Do 17s were shot down while No. 54's surviving Spitfires destroyed one of the escorting Bf 109s.

Deere had now been shot down (or blown-up) seven times. It was obviously time for a change while he was still ahead. On 3 September, No. 54 left Hornchurch for Catterick where Deere, with a Bar to his D.F.C., became a controller.

The following year, on 23 February 1941, No. 54 returned to Hornchurch. On that day, No. 41 Squadron flew up to Catterick and turned its Spitfire IIAs over to No. 54. With these, the squadron flew its first offensive sweep over Northern France when it joined with No. 64 Squadron as escort for 12 Blenheims raiding Calais.

After the *Luftwaffe* gave up large-scale daylight bombing and began night attacks on British cities, only small forces of enemy aircraft ventured over the British Isles. Most of these were bomb-carrying Bf 109s relying on their speed to evade interception. The toll of enemy aircraft dropped considerably and, in December 1940, the first steps were taken to open the offensive against the *Luftwaffe* over its own airfields.

At first, these fighter sweeps brought a reaction from the enemy fighter units but this fell off and

1

2

squadrons toured the Pas-de-Calais with nothing but *flak* damage to show for their efforts. It was then decided that fighter sweeps should be in support of a small bomber force attacking targets which the *Luftwaffe* would have to defend. Blenheims were used for this role although, on some occasions, the new four-motor Short Stirling heavy-bombers provided the bombing complement. The latter presented a large target for the *flak* and Stirlings were withdrawn after suffering damage from the highly accurate 88-mm anti-aircraft artillery of the defences.

Enemy fighters appeared from time to time, often with the advantage of height as, like the Messerschmitts during the Battle of Britain, the escorting fighter squadrons found themselves tied to the bomber force. It was only too easy to lose their charges in the clouds over the French coast. The answer was to provide high cover for the close escort squadrons and these operations (known as 'Circuses') became larger as the year wore on. Sometimes as many as 15 squadrons of fighters would be over France as part of an operation which resulted in a dozen Blenheims dropping their modest load on a power station.

During March, the squadron claimed seven enemy fighters over France and continued to take part in 'sweeps' for most of 1941. On one patrol over the Pas-de-Calais, Flight Lieutenant George Gribble, DFC radioed that his engine had cut and he was seen to bale out 12 miles off the English coast. Despite searches he was not picked up and the squadron lost the last of its pre-war pilots.

In November 1941, a move was made to the other end of the country. Castletown, between Wick and Thurso, was the main fighter station for the defence of Scapa Flow naval base in the Orkneys and the Pentland Firth used by shipping plying between the East Coast ports and the Atlantic. The weather was cold and flying made hazardous by cloud-covered mountains. Enemy aircraft were few and restricted themselves to high-altitude reconnaissance. It was with some relief that No. 54 left its aircraft in the north and travelled to Wellingore in Lincolnshire. The personnel were given embarkation leave and tropical kit collected. Squadrons had been leaving for the Middle East for several months but No. 54 Squadron was in for a surprise.

Fifty-Four goes Down Under

The unprecedented wave of success following the entry of Japan into the war had resulted in the unexpected arrival of enemy forces within striking distance of Australia. Deprived of support from the United States Navy's Pacific Fleet as a result of the attack on Pearl Harbor and, three days later, of a small British

3

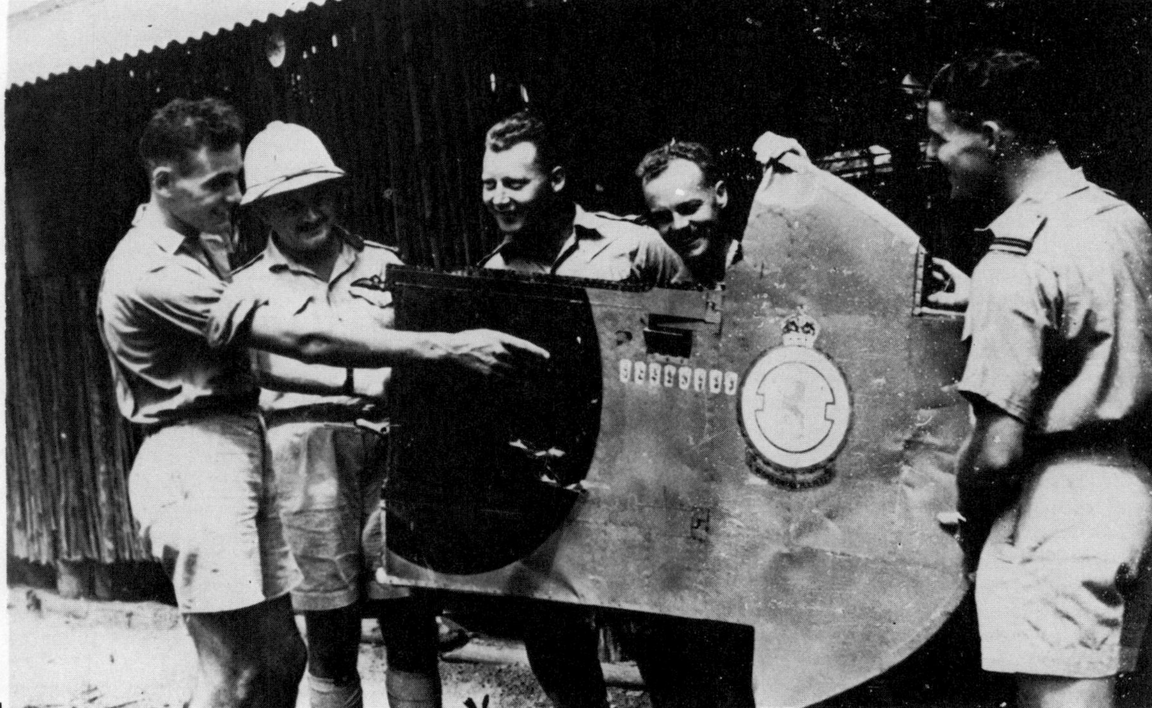
4

1 The Commanding Officer's Spitfire MA863 is pushed into its camouflaged dispersal at Darwin. (*Photo: RAAF MH.52831.*)
2 Camouflage netting throws an unusual pattern on a dispersed Spitfire at Darwin. The red centre of the roundel was removed from British aircraft operating in the Far East due to its resemblance to the Japanese 'Hinomaru'. (*Photo: RAAF MH.52822.*)
3 Spitfire BR536 'DL-H', better known to No. 54 Squadron as 'Butch II', being salvaged after landing on the sea on 2 May 1943. (*Photo: RAAF MH.52811.*)
4 No. 54 Squadron's score-board was the wing-tip of a shot-down Mitsubishi A6M2 fighter. Victories were indicated by beermugs. (*Photo: No. 54 Squadron collection.*)

Fleet sunk off Malaya, the Australian forces were faced with the task of defending Northern Australia from Imperial Japanese air and sea forces now operating from New Guinea and the Dutch East Indies.

The bulk of the Royal Australian Air Force's first-line aircraft had been sent to Singapore for the defence of Malaya and by the end of February 1942 most had been lost in action. When a Japanese carrier force attacked Darwin on 19 February, air defence was in the hands of 10 U.S. Army Air Force Curtiss P-40s (later known as Warhawks) en route to Java. All were destroyed along with 13 other aircraft. Another Japanese air raid on 3 March was undisturbed by fighters and 16 flying-boats were destroyed in the harbour at Broome and eight landplanes on the airfield and in the air. It was not until 17 March that fighters reached Darwin—a squadron of U.S.A.A.F. P-40s of the 49th Pursuit Group, to be joined in April by the other two squadrons of the same group.

The Australian Government, alarmed at the situation and fearing that Japanese landings would take place in the Darwin area—whose communications with the rest of Australia were precarious—took decisive action. During May, Dr. Evatt, Minister for External Affairs, visited London and sought the transfer of Spitfires to Australia. Mr. Churchill was sympathetic to the request and it was arranged that three fighter squadrons should be sent from the U.K. Two obvious candidates were Nos. 452 and 457 Squadrons, both Australian-manned. The third squadron nominated was No. 54. Each was to take 16 Spitfires with them and five Spitfires per month were to be supplied as replacements.

In June, the squadron was kitted-out for overseas service but, for various reasons, nearly two-thirds of the personnel were ineligible for overseas postings and were replaced. On 18 June, embarkation took place at Liverpool and the convoy sailed from the Mersey two days later. Arriving at Freetown (Sierra Leone) without incident, no shore leave was allowed; after four days at anchor, the convoy sailed again, arriving at Durban on 20 July. Having partaken of Durban's famous hospitality, the squadron sailed on 26 July and docked at Melbourne on 13 August. The personnel disembarked to be housed on the Agricultural Show Ground in very primitive conditions. Ten days later, they moved to Richmond, New South Wales, where they were to receive their Spitfires.

Unfortunately, a shipment of 42 Spitfires on the high seas had been diverted to the Middle East and such flying as was done was in R.A.A.F. Commonwealth Aircraft Wirraways and Ryan STM-2s. On 21 September, the first Spitfires reached Australia and were taken to Laverton, near Melbourne, for assembly. There they were joined by a detachment from No. 54 eager to get hold of some operational aircraft at last. On 13 October, six Spitfires left for Richmond but had to put down at Wagga Wagga due to bad weather. It then proceeded to rain for eight days until a break appeared that enabled the fighters to press on. By the time the squadron was declared operational on 2 December, it had revised its opinion of the Australian weather as depicted in travel posters. It had also learned more about the local geography and had been distressed to find that their operational area was more remote from the famous Sydney playground of Bondi Beach than they had hoped.

The main ground party embarked in a Dutch transport on 12 January and sailed for Darwin, arriving on 25 January. Another party set out by rail and voted the New South Wales Railway carriages the most uncomfortable in the world. Arriving at Adelaide they transferred to cattle trucks which had not even been cleaned out and regretted leaving the 'luxury' of their coaches. From Alice Springs to Birdum there was no railway at all and the gap was filled by a four-day trip in trucks without any seats. The final stretch of rail travel was in more cattle-trucks. By the time the sea party arrived in the vessel they had dubbed *Altmark II*,* the squadron was all in favour of giving Darwin to the Japanese.

The air party took-off from Richmond on 14 January, escorted by a Beaufighter, together with a Lockheed Lodestar with maintenance crews and spares. After night stops at Mildura, Alice Springs and Daly Waters, they reached Darwin on 17 January and flew the first patrols on 28 January, eight months after the plans to place the squadron at Darwin had begun.

6 February 1943 was the day when No. 54 saw a Japanese aircraft at last. Flight Lieutenant R. E. Foster in a Spitfire VC (BS181) and Flight Sergeant Mahoney (BR495) were 'scrambled' to intercept a Japanese reconnaissance aircraft plotted 35 miles w.n.w. of Cape van Diemen. Foster sighted and attacked a two-motor Mitsubishi Ki-46 (Allied code-name 'Dinah') which was seen by both pilots to hit the waves in flames.

Operating conditions were primitive and when the Wing Leader, Wing Commander C. R. Caldwell (who had led No. 112 Squadron with great success in the Middle East) led a flight of six Spitfires to cover a Dutch freighter, his arrival at the emergency landing ground at Drysdale River Mission for the night resulted in his tipping-up on the rough surface. In the absence of any repair facilities, the bent propeller was beaten back to approximately the correct shape with a nine-pound hammer and BS295 flown back to base.

The largest force of Japanese aircraft seen since the arrival of the Spitfire squadrons crossed the coast on 2 March when 16 of the enemy attacked Coomalie airstrip. Two sections of No. 54 Squadron intercepted this raid 30 miles off Point Charles and destroyed three; a fourth being shot down by anti-aircraft gunners.

A much heavier raid took place on 15 March. About 22 medium-bombers with strong fighter escort arrived over Darwin and were engaged by the whole wing in an action which was reminiscent of the mass *Luftwaffe* raids during the Battle of Britain. No. 54 provided top cover and engaged the 'Zekes' (Mitsubishi A6Ms). Three fell to the guns of Flight Lieutenant Norwood (flying BR544), Flying Officer Mawer (BS305) and Flight Sergeant Biggs (BR536), and Flight Lieutenant Foster destroyed a 'Betty' (Mitsubishi G4M) bomber. Seven enemy aircraft were destroyed and seven more were claimed as damaged for the loss of four Spitfires. No. 54 lost Sergeant A. E. Cooper (in AR620) and Flight Sergeant F. L. Varney (AR619) who force-landed on a beach and was fatally injured.

After a quiet April, the next month opened with another heavy raid. On 2 May, a radar station on Bathurst Island located an enemy force 160 miles from Darwin, whose controller then ordered all three squadrons into the air. Led by Caldwell, the wing assembled 33 Spitfires but failed to gain a height advantage until the raiders were over Darwin. No. 54 was again directed against the fighter escort while the Australian squadrons closed with the retiring bombers. Squadron Leader Gibbs led the R.A.F. Spitfires in an almost vertical dive on the 'Zekes' and saw his first target burst into flames. Taken by surprise, the Japanese fighters broke formation and the sky was filled with diving and turning aircraft. Flying Officer Farries (in BR239) accounted for a second 'Zeke' but, in turn, was shot down and took to his rubber dinghy. He was rescued after 5½ hours by a Supermarine Walrus amphibian.

The Australian squadrons were simultaneously attacking the bombers which were defended by even more fighters. Thus, when the action was broken off due to fuel shortage, enemy losses totalled eight destroyed, four probables and eight damaged. Five Spitfires had gone down and three of their pilots were in their dinghies awaiting rescue. Sixteen minutes after the attack began, Caldwell recalled his scattered fighters and headed for home, now a long way off. Though within the normal capacity of Spitfires, the chase had resulted in abnormal consumption of fuel and an adverse wind did nothing to help. Five aircraft ran out of fuel and force-landed, one in the sea, and three more suffered engine failure causing a fatal crash. This brought the total number lost during the day to eight with six more force-landed and awaiting recovery.

At this point, an astonishing series of events left the squadron baffled. General MacArthur—who had been appointed Supreme Commander in the South-West Pacific after his defeat in the Philippines—had been criticized for the optimistic communiques issuing from his headquarters. Presumably because no U.S. forces were involved and Darwin was remote from his main preoccupations, a communique was issued to redress the balance. It announced baldly that Spitfires defending Darwin had engaged a Japanese bomber force and suffered heavy casualties. The squadrons involved were staggered, newspapers throughout the world reported that Spitfires were 'outclassed' and R.A.A.F. Headquarters was outraged.

An amending press release mentioned 'bad weather' as contributing to the losses, another obvious untruth, and the men of the Spitfire squadrons suspected that it was a plot to boost the morale of the U.S. fighter squadrons in New Guinea who were having to cope with Japanese fighters while flying obsolescent Bell P-39s (Airacobras) and P-40s, neither of which were a match for the 'Zeke'.

The Japanese reacted predictably, claiming 21 Spitfires shot down without loss to themselves!

During June, two more big raids took place. On 20 June, about 40 'Bettys' and 'Zekes' bombed Winnellie airfield without causing much damage and a running fight took place. A second formation of 19 bombers attacked Darwin, again with little damage. The squadron destroyed five bombers and one fighter without loss and the wing accounted for a total of 9 bombers and 5 fighters for the loss of two pilots of No. 452 Squadron.

The second raid was directed against the Liberator base at Fenton on 30 June. A force of 27 bombers and

* After the notorious *Altmark*, a supply tanker taking *KM. Graf Spee's* captured British merchant seamen to Germany in 1940—Editor.

23 fighters were once more detected by the watchful radar stations and 38 Spitfires were waiting for them. Nos. 54 and 457 Squadrons attacked the enemy bombers but due to a misunderstanding of radio orders were followed by No. 452 which was to have occupied the fighter escort. This resulted in the loss of 3 Spitfires during an action that ended in the destruction of 6 enemy bombers and 2 fighters. Three more Spitfires were lost in forced landings due to engine failure, the dust and the frequent use of high power settings having played havoc with the elderly Merlins. Three Liberators were destroyed by bombs.

Wear and tear on No. 54's aircraft was increased by the lack of replacements and when 27 bombers came over on 6 July, only seven Spitfires managed to reach the enemy. Four bombers were shot down but Flight Sergeant Wickman (in JG731) was shot down in the bush whence he was rescued and a second Spitfire (BR495) force-landed and was written-off.

This raid marked the end of major Japanese raids on Darwin and for the rest of the war, the Spitfire wing found few targets. In March 1944 No. 54 at last received more modern aircraft with the arrival of Spitfire VIIIs. Nos. 452 and 457 left No. 1 Fighter Wing on 30 June for New Guinea and were replaced by two new R.A.F. squadrons, Nos. 548 and 549. A few 'sweeps' were flown over the nearest Japanese bases but the range was too great for the Spitfires to go further afield and the wing spent the rest of the war flying defensive patrols.

Japan's surrender resulted in the breaking-up of No. 1 Fighter Wing. The aircraft were ferried to Oakey in Queensland and the personnel of the last ground party left Darwin without regret on 16 September, 1945. Melbourne Cricket Ground accommodated the R.A.F. men until 30 October when they left for Sydney and a ship for home. Next day the orderly room closed down and the activities of the R.A.F. fighter squadrons in Australia came to an end.

Return to Fighter Command

At Chilbolton in Hampshire, No. 183 Squadron had been equipped with Hawker Tempest II fighters as part of the fighter defences of the U.K. On 15 November 1945, this squadron was renumbered as No. 54 Squadron.

The Tempest II was a variant of the successful Tempest V used widely in Europe for the last year of

No. 54 Squadron's aerobatic team pioneered the use of coloured smoke. (*Photo: Flight International 24640.*)

the war. The squadron's Tempests differed in being fitted with Bristol Centaurus radial engines which gave them a top speed of 440 m.p.h. at 15,000 feet. Armed with four 20-mm cannon, they could also carry up to 2,000-lb of bombs or rockets. With long-range tanks they had a range of 1,640 miles and No. 54 could have used them very effectively a year before but the day of the piston-engined fighter was drawing to a close.

In June 1946, the squadron left its war-built airfield for the permanent station at Odiham (Hampshire) not far away. Here, in October 1946, No. 54 converted to de Havilland Vampires. These twin-boom fighters also equipped the other two squadrons at Odiham (Nos. 72 and 247) to form the first Vampire wing. Its 3,100-lb static thrust de Havilland Goblin engine gave the Vampire a speed of 540 m.p.h. at 20,000 feet and a climb of 4,200 feet per minute.

In April 1948, long-range Vampire F.3s were received in time for No. 54 to make history. A flight of Vampires made the first crossing of the Atlantic by R.A.F. jets. Escorted by a trio of Mosquito PR.34s—flown by Transport Command crews—six Vampires (VT863, 864, 868, 869, 871 and 873) left Odiham on 1 July 1948 bound for Stornoway in the Outer Hebrides. Their pilots were Squadron Leader R. W. Oxpring (No. 54's Commanding Officer) and Flight Lieutenants E. W. Wright and F. G. Woolley, Pilots I. S. Evans and W. Wood and Pilot II R. J. Skinner, the last three indicative of the short-lived system used for designating non-commissioned pilots at this time.

Persistent headwinds of between 75 and 146 knots held the Vampires at Stornoway until 12 July when they crossed to Meeks Field in Iceland—a Coastal Command Avro Lancaster and a USAF Boeing SB-17 Flying Fortress providing air-sea-rescue cover. An attempt to push on to Bluie West I in Greenland after refuelling was thwarted by a faulty warning light in the leader's aircraft which caused the flight to put back to Iceland. On 14 July, the Vampires made it to Greenland and on to Goose Bay, Labrador, where they gave a display to the isolated base next day. On 16 July the flight continued through Mount Joli, St. Hubert and on to Trenton, Ontario where the Vampires were based for displays at Oshawa and Toronto.

Their next destination was Andrews Field, Washington, D.C., where they arrived on 24 July. This was followed by a visit to Greenville, South Carolina, for tactical exercises with U.S.A.F. fighter squadrons before heading north to Mitchel Field, New York, for displays at the opening of New York's new international airport at Idlewild (now John F. Kennedy International Airport). Returning to Trenton on 10 August, the flight departed for home on 16 August by

1

the same airfields used on the outward trip. Bad weather caused some delays, but on 25 August the six Vampires landed at Stornoway. One suffered engine failure there and had to be left behind as the remaining five flew back to their base at Odiham on the following day to complete a highly successful exercise.

With the arrival of Vampire FB.5s in October 1949, the squadron acquired the fighter-bomber version of the Vampire but by 1952 the type was replaced in the U.K. by Gloster Meteor F.8s, No. 54 converting in April to the larger but faster twin-jet aircraft. These were flown for three years until the arrival of Hawker Hunters in March 1955. The squadron lost no time in forming an aerobatic display team with its new swept-wing fighters and performed at several air events during the summer. Then, in September 1955, the squadron received the more potent Mark 4s.

By 1962, the squadron's traditional defensive role was coming to an end. No. 38 Group, responsible for tactical support for the Army, was to be given a ground-attack wing and Nos. 1 and 54 Squadrons were chosen. The unfortunate fact that No. 54 was to join Transport Command was borne with stoicism though it was with not inconsiderable relief that Transport Command was renamed Air Support Command some years later.

The Hunters' two-fold tasks were close-support for the ground units using cannon and rockets, and fighter cover for the transport aircraft if required. To carry out these roles, the squadron had re-equipped with fighter (ground-attack) Hunter FGA.9s in March 1960, aircraft which had been modified from Mark 6 fighters by the provision of rocket racks and attachment points for long-range tanks, bombs or rocket packs.

The two squadrons remained based in the U.K. but were highly mobile, taking part in exercises throughout Europe and the Middle East. No. 54's Hunters were to be seen in the snow-covered airfields of Northern Norway and the sandy airstrips of Libya.

The year 1969 marked a turning point for many fighter squadrons—and No. 54 was no exception. The Hunters were due for replacement. By a fortunate coincidence the type was in great demand by foreign air forces, the manufacturers being busily engaged in

2

3

1/2 Hunter F.1s of No. 54 Squadron aerobatic team in 1955. (*Photo: Hawker Siddeley Aviation P.494/55, Flight International 32026.*)

3 The tarmac at Odiham in 1955 with a row of No. 54 Squadron Hunters behind a line of Meteor NF.14s of No. 46 Squadron. (*Photo: Flight International 32027.*)

1

2

3

buying back every airframe they could locate. No. 1 Squadron was converted to Hawker Siddeley Harrier VTOL (vertical take-off and landing) fighters and No. 54 was scheduled to follow early in 1970.

A change of plan resulted in the remaining Hunters and crews being transferred to No. 4 Squadron in Germany though they remained at West Raynham (Norfolk) as the U.K. Echelon of No. 4 Squadron. On the date this occurred, a new No. 54 Squadron was formed at Coningsby (Lincolnshire), home of the British-based Air Support Command McDonnell Douglas Phantoms. Crews had been trained by the resident No. 228 Operational Conversion Unit and on 1 September 1969, No. 54 resumed its place in the Command with FGR Mark 2s, the role prefix denoting fighter/ground-attack/reconnaissance.

Compared to the Hunter, the Phantom was massive, with the ability to fly long distances and carry vast loads at very high speeds. In December 1969, a pair of the squadron's Phantoms flew to Singapore, refuelling at Malta and Masirah on the way. This was followed by long-range flights around the U.K. refuelling from Handley Page Victor tankers.

With the Phantom cleared for 15-hours continuous running on its Rolls-Royce Spey engines, it was decided to go for the England-Singapore record. The Royal Aero Club, responsible for monitoring all British record-breaking flights, was brought into the picture and arranged for its officials to be on hand to record times. The flight began over Hornchurch, the observer using London Airport's radar to check the time of departure from this point, chosen to keep within the 50-kilometre radius of Hyde Park Corner that constituted London for international record attempts. Squadron Leader John Nevill and Flight Lieutenant Jim Straughan were first off (in XV409) at 11:49 on 19 May 1970 followed by Flight Lieutenants Walmsley and Spencer in XV419. The pair of Phantoms were checked out over Hornchurch and rendezvoused with

1 Hunters of No. 54 Squadron taxiing at Odiham in 1955; note the lightning flash on tail of the flight leader's aircraft. (*Photo: Flight International 32035.*)

2 A Hunter FGA.9 of No. 54 Squadron taxies in at Andoya airfield in Northern Norway during a NATO exercise in 1966. (*Photo: Ministry of Defence PRB.35066.*)

3 Hunter FGA.9 XG254 on the apron at West Raynham in 1960. (*Photo: Minstry of Defence PRB.22034.*)

their first Victor tanker from Marham soon afterwards to 'top up'. Another hook-up near Nice from an accompanying Victor and the two aircraft headed for Cyprus where a major refuelling took place. Over Turkey and Iran and down the Persian Gulf to another rendezvous with Victors over Masirah off the Arabian coast in darkness. A pair of Victors from Gan in the Indian Ocean formed the next relay station, refuelling being delayed slightly by a thunderstorm which spectacularly illuminated the aircraft with St. Elmo's Fire. Near Sumatra, a high-speed descent began and an English Electric Lightning of No. 74 Squadron intercepted the Phantoms, leading them over Tengah where the official observer timed the arrival. The elapsed time came to 14 hours, 8 minutes, 40 seconds for the 8,680 mile flight. The average speed was 603 m.p.h. and this included the drop to half-speed during refuelling operations. It was a vivid reminder of the range and mobility of Air Support Command's tactical squadrons.

In June 1970, the squadron sent 10 Phantoms over the same route to take part in exercise 'Bersatu Padu' in Singapore and Malaysia where they cooperated with units of the Fleet Air Arm, Royal Australian Air Force, Royal New Zealand Air Force, Royal Malaysian Air Force and ground troops from five countries.

The jump from 300 miles in a Sopwith Pup to halfway across the world in a Phantom in a relatively short time required the acquisition of many new skills and techniques. But if the equipment is unrecognizable to those first fighter pilots, nevertheless they would doubtless detect in today's Phantom pilots the spirit they saw in their fellow pilots on the Western Front when the fighter squadrons were born.

1

2

3

1 Phantom FGR.2 XV477 refuelling from a Victor tanker; note arrester hook fitted as standard to R.A.F. Phantoms. (*Photo: Ministry of Defence TN5803.*)

2 Phantoms refuel from a Victor tanker of No. 214 Squadron in preparation for a non-stop deployment to Singapore. (*Photo: Ministry of Defence TN5839.*)

3 Phantom XV419 on final approach to Tengah airfield, Singapore. (*Photo: R.A.F. Tengah.*)

SQUADRON BASES

Castle Bromwich, Warwickshire	15 May 1916
London Colney, Hertfordshire	22 December 1916
St. Omer, France	24 December 1916
Bertangles, France	26 December 1916
Flez, France	23 April 1917
Bray Dunes, France	18 June 1917
Leffrinckoucke, France	16 July 1917
Teteghem, France	8 September 1917
Bruay, France	6 December 1917
La Houssoye, France	18 December 1917
Flez, France	1 January 1918
Champien, France	22 March 1918
Bertangles, France	24 March 1918
Conteville, France	28 March 1918
Clairmarais, France	7 April 1918
Caffiers, France	29 April 1918
St. Omer, France	1 June 1918
Vignacourt, France	11 June 1918
Boisdinghem, France	16 June 1918
Lièttres, France	30 June 1918
Touquin, France	14 July 1918
Fienvillers, France	4 August 1918
Avèsnes-le-Compte, France	25 August 1918
Rély, France	17 October 1918
Merchin, France	24 October 1918
Yatesbury, Wiltshire	17 February 1919 to 25 October 1919
Hornchurch, Essex	15 January 1930
Upavon, Wiltshire	28 May 1931
Hornchurch, Essex	20 June 1931
Rochford, Essex	28 October 1939
Hornchurch, Essex	3 November 1939
Rochford, Essex	17 November 1939
Hornchurch, Essex	2 December 1939
Rochford, Essex	16 December 1939
Hornchurch, Essex	29 December 1939
Rochford, Essex	16 January 1940
Hornchurch, Essex	14 February 1940
Rochford, Essex	23 March 1940
Hornchurch, Essex	20 April 1940
Catterick, Yorkshire	28 May 1940
Hornchurch, Essex	4 June 1940
Rochford, Essex	25 June 1940
Hornchurch, Essex	24 July 1940
Catterick, Yorkshire	28 July 1940
Hornchurch, Essex	8 August 1940
Catterick, Yorkshire	3 September 1940
Hornchurch, Essex	23 February 1941
Southend, Essex	31 March 1941
Hornchurch, Essex	20 May 1941
Debden, Essex	11 June 1941
Hornchurch, Essex	13 June 1941
Martlesham Heath, Suffolk	4 August 1941
Castletown, Caithness	17 November 1941
Wellingore, Lincolnshire	1 June 1942
Embarked for Australia	18 June 1942
Arrived Melbourne	13 August 1942
Richmond, Australia	24 August 1942
Darwin/Night Cliff, Australia	17 January 1943 (Aircraft) 25 January 1943 (Sea party)
Darwin/Livingstone, Australia	8 June 1944
Darwin Civil, Australia	21 October 1944
Melbourne, Australia	23 September 1945 to 31 October 1945
Chilbolton, Hampshire	15 November 1945
Odiham, Hampshire	28 June 1946
Molesworth, Northamptonshire	5 September 1946
Odiham, Hampshire	30 September 1946
Stradishall, Suffolk	13 July 1959
Waterbeach, Cambridgeshire	20 November 1961
West Raynham, Norfolk	14 August 1963 to 1 September 1969
Coningsby, Lincolnshire	1 September 1969

COMMANDING OFFICERS

Major K.K.Horn	15 August 1916
Major R.S.Maxwell	29 November 1917
S/Ldr. W.E.G.Bryant MBE	15 January 1930
S/Ldr. S.L.G.Pope DFC AFC	7 March 1932
S/Ldr. I.M.Rodney	21 January 1933
S/Ldr. G.D.Daly DFC	4 January 1934
S/Ldr. C.A.Bouchier OBE DFC	23 August 1936
S/Ldr. H.M.Pearson	2 April 1938
S/Ldr. E.A.Douglas-Jones	1 May 1940
S/Ldr. J.A.Leathart	24 May 1940
S/Ldr. D.O.Finlay	27 August 1940
S/Lrd. T.P.R.Dunworth	7 September 1940
S/Ldr. R.F.Boyd DFC and Bar	25 December 1940
S/Ldr. N.Orton DFC	19 July 1941
S/Ldr. F.D.S.Scott-Malden	19 September 1941
S/Ldr. P.W.Hartley	31 December 1941
S/Ldr. E.M.Gibbs	10 April 1942
S/Ldr. R.B.Newton DFC	11 January 1944
S/Ldr. S.Linnard DFC	27 July 1944
S/Ldr. J.B.A.Nicholas	1 July 1945
S/Ldr. F.W.M.Jenson	1 December 1945
S/Ldr. M.D.Lyne AFC	10 October 1946
S/Ldr. F.J.Howell	12 January 1948
S/Ldr. R.W.Oxpring DFC and Two Bars	12 May 1948
S/Ldr. E.W.Wright DFC DFM	29 November 1948
S/Ldr. A.C.Rawlinson DFC and Bar	13 June 1949
S/Ldr. E.Plumtree	10 October 1949
S/Ldr. P.J.Kelley	4 September 1951
S/Ldr. W.M.Sizer DFC and Bar	2 November 1953
S/Ldr. W.J.Stacey	9 January 1956
S/Ldr. I.A.N.Worby	3 February 1958
S/Ldr. W.D.Dickinson	1 June 1960
S/Ldr. C.P.Francis	9 April 1962
S/Ldr. D.Harcourt-Smith DFC	14 August 1963
S/Ldr. A.Neale	23 August 1965
S/Ldr. J.T.Hall	13 July 1967
S/Ldr. R.M.Austin	22 March 1969
W/Cdr. R.J.Bannard	1 September 1969
W/Cdr. H.Davidson	24 July 1971

SQUADRON EQUIPMENT

Period of Use & Typical Serial and Code Letters

Aircraft	Period of Use	Serial and Code
B.E.2c	August 1916 to December 1916	—
Avro 504	September 1916 to December 1916	—
Sopwith Pup	October 1916 to December 1917	A6211
Sopwith Camel	December 1917 to February 1919	B7320 (P)
Armstrong Whitworth Siskin IIIDC	January 1930 to December 1930	J7146
Bristol Bulldog IIA	April 1930 to September 1936	K1611
Gloster Gauntlet II	September 1936 to May 1937	K5313
Gloster Gladiator I	April 1937 to April 1939	K8014
Supermarine Spitfire I	March 1939 to February 1941	K9901 (DL-D)
Supermarine Spitfire IIA	February 1941 to May 1941 August 1941	P7618 (KL-Z)
Supermarine Spitfire IIB	November 1941 to March 1942	P8697
Supermarine Spitfire VA	May 1941 to August 1941	R7279 (KL-S)
Supermarine Spitfire VB	June 1941 to November 1941	AA761
	March 1942 to May 1942	AA761
Supermarine Spitfire VC	September 1942 to May 1944	BS164 (K)
Supermarine Spitfire VIII	March 1944 to September 1945	A58-428 (B)
Hawker Tempest II	November 1945 to October 1946	MW755 (HF-W)
de Havilland Vampire F.1	October 1946 to April 1948	TG298 (HF-F)
de Havilland Vampire F.3	April 1948 to November 1949	VT874 (C)
de Havilland Vampire FB.5	October 1949 to April 1952	VV630
Gloster Meteor F.8	April 1952 to March 1955	WH471 (Z)
Hawker Hunter F.1	March 1955 to October 1955	WW610 (A)
Hawker Hunter F.4	September 1955 to January 1957	XE661 (B)
Hawker Hunter F.6	January 1957 to March 1960	XF509 (M)
Hawker Hunter FGA.9	March 1960 to September 1969	XF517 (V)
McDonnell Douglas Phantom FGR.2	September 1969 to date	XV477 (477)

1

1 Supermarine Spitfire IIA 07666 carried the emblem of the (later Royal) Observer Corps and served with No. 41 Squadron from November 1940 until February 1941 when it was transferred to No. 54 Squadron. On 20 April 1941, Pilot Officer Stokoe had just shot down a Messerschmitt Bf 110 when he was attacked by Bf 109s and P7666 went down into the English Channel in flames, the pilot being picked up by a drifter.

2 Sopwith Pup B1704 was built by the Standard Motor Co Ltd. No. 54 Squadron's Pups do not appear to have carried squadron identification marks at any time.

3 Bristol Bulldog IIA K1605 carried No. 54 Squadron's original yellow band behind the roundel only. It was struck off charge on 7 June 1934.

2

3

1

1 McDonnell Douglas Phantom FGR.2 XV437 originally carried the last three digits of its serial on the fin but No. 54 Squadron gave its aircraft letter codes in August 1971. Arrester hooks are fitted as standard on R.A.F. Phantoms.

2 Hawker Tempest F.2 MW774 was in service with No. 183 Squadron when it became No. 54 Squadron in November 1945 and served till December 1946.

3 De Havilland Vampire FB.5 VZ115 was built by English Electric Co at Samlesbury and delivered to No. 54 Squadron in October 1949 to replace a Vampire F.3. In March 1952, it was transferred to No. 112 Squadron and crashed on 17 March 1953 in Germany.

2

3

No.111 Squadron

One of a pair of Bristol M.1 Bs used by No. 111 Squadron seen before shipment; Note the mounting of the Vickers gun on the wing root; production M.1 Cs had their guns fitted on the fuselage in from of the cockpit. (*Photo: Ministry of Defence H.999.*)

No. 111 (Fighter) Squadron occupies a unique position in being the only squadron whose number became widely known to the general public. Through its connection with the formation team of black Hawker Hunters that appeared widely in the 1950s, 'Treble One' was for many years the world's most famous aerobatic team.

The origins of the squadron go back to 1917 and the Sinai Desert. Since the outbreak of the First World War, Imperial and Turkish troops had faced each other between British-occupied Egypt and Turkish-governed Palestine. For most of the time, both sides remained static, shortage of troops and supply difficulties precluding a major attack. In 1917, the front line lay along the southern borders of Palestine, supplied by a thin coastal lifeline.

Air support for the Army was rationed to a small number of mainly obsolete aircraft. Opposition had been met from German fighters and it was decided that a fighter squadron should be formed not only to combat these and also to restrict the operations of enemy reconnaissance aircraft which frequently outperformed the few defending aircraft able to reach them.

On 1 August 1917, No. 111 was formally formed in the desert at Deir-el-Belah and Major A. Shekleton arrived to command. He had already commanded a fighter squadron in France and was joined by two flight commanders and some men from No. 14 Squadron which had been operating what fighters were available on the Suez front. A Bristol Scout, two de Havilland D.H.2s and two Vickers F.B.19s were provided and a week after formation seven pilots arrived to fly them. On 8 August, Second Lieutenant R. C. Steele made the squadron's first war flight by escorting a reconnaissance aircraft. His D.H.2 engaged two enemy aircraft bent on attacking his charge and one was seen to fall out of control.

A pair of Bristol M.1B monoplanes arrived next and were allotted to 'A' Flight which was completed by nine Vickers Bullets (as the F.B.19s were dubbed). Meanwhile, 'B' Flight flew the D.H.2 pusher scouts. During September, six Bristol Fighters were flown in from Egypt and gunners taken on strength to complete the squadron before it was allotted to the newly-formed 40th Army Wing.

The multiplicity of types made maintenance work difficult. With Clerget and Le Rhone air-cooled rotary and Rolls-Royce Falcon water-cooled upright-Vee engines to look after, mechanics were hard pressed. The Bristol Monoplanes were two of four prototypes built as M.1Bs. The squadron did not receive the production M.1Cs which were sent to Mesopotamia and Salonika and which proved popular because of their speed and manoeuvrability. The D.H.2 had entered service at the end of 1915 and began operations in France in February 1916 as the R.F.C.'s first single-seat fighter. Only a dozen Vickers F.B.19s saw operational service, all in Palestine or Salonika. It was the two-seat Bristol Fighters on which No. 111 mainly had to depend.

On 8 October, four Bristol Fighters were sent to patrol in pairs in the hope of intercepting enemy reconnaissance aircraft. Second Lieutenant R. C. Steele with Lieutenant J. J. Lloyd-Williams as observer was flying A7194 at 15,000 feet in the region of Sharia accompanied by Lieutenants Parnell-McGarry and Marks (in A7190) when two enemy reconnaissance aircraft escorted by two fighters were sighted. Parnell-McGarry chased the two-seaters while Steele engaged the pair of Albatros D.IIIs. After several bursts of fire, one of the Albatroses dived away and Steele got on the tail of the second. The enemy spun and dived steeply, closely followed by the Bristol which had no difficulty in following. The Albatros landed in the British lines and the pilot, *Oberleutnant* Ditmar, was taken into custody by Anzac cavalry, thoroughly shaken by the fact that for the first time his fighter had been unable to outdive a British aircraft.

Enemy suspicion that their superiority in performance was at an end were confirmed on 15 October when Steele intercepted a reconnaissance aircraft and shot it down. Such flights by the enemy dwindled while the Bristols were increasingly used for reconnaissance missions on which B.E.s and R.E.8s would have been vulnerable. The Vickers Bullets were used for escort duties while the D.H.2s engaged in machine-gunning ground targets. More Bristol fighters were received in October and two flights formed to replace the Bristol Monoplanes and Vickers Bullets. A new type to arrive was the S.E.5 a single-seater which was a potent aircraft.

The arrival of a *staffel* of new Rumplers was reported by the intelligence network and Major-General Sir Sefton Brancker, commander of the Middle East Brigade, despatched 26 bombers to attack the enemy airfield, escorted by No. 111's fighters. Cavalry captured the airfield two days later and found about a dozen new Rumplers wrecked and burnt.

Major Shekleton was promoted to command 40th Wing and Major F. W. Stent took over the squadron. 'A' Flight moved forward to Julis on 17 November

1

2

3

1 A Vickers F.B.19 Mk. II serving with No. 111 Squadron in Palestine in late 1917. (*Photo: Ministry of Defence H.1274.*)

2 An S.E.5a displays the squadron's identification stripe on the rear fuselage. In the background are transportable aircraft shelters. (*Photo: Ministry of Defence H.1875.*)

3 No. 111's Nieuports were armed with two Lewis guns in place of the normal single gun used on the Western Front, the extra weight not penalising the aircraft to the same extent when facing enemy aircraft of lower performance than in France. Note the interconnecting clamp to the periscopic sight and the twin firing cables. (*Photo: I.W.M. Q.69446.*)

where it was joined by the rest of the squadron on 1 December. No hangars were erected as it was expected that a further move was imminent and the enemy took the opportunity of sending six aircraft over in the early morning to attack the airfield. By the time they had located the target, personnel had dispersed into the desert while defensive fire was put up by the Lewis guns in the rear cockpits of the Bristols. Each side did no damage to the other and next day 30 British aircraft attacked the enemy airfield after which no further raids were experienced.

Jerusalem was captured in early December and the Bristols were engaged in attacking ground troops for the first time. Retreating enemy columns were machine-gunned but after two of the Bristols were badly damaged by ground fire it was decided that they were too valuable to risk in such actions and were retained for air fighting, there being few replacements available in the Middle East.

The enemy continued to suffer at the hands of the Bristol crews. On 12 December, Captain R. M. Drummond was escorting two R.E.8s when three Albatros D.IIIs appeared from the direction of Nablus. Closing on his charges, Drummond circled them until one Albatros attacked. Corporal Knowles emptied a drum from his Lewis into it and 30 rounds from the pilot's front gun caused the enemy fighter to spin down. The Bristol followed but was attacked by the two remaining Albatroses which were kept at bay by Knowles' rear gun until one turned away and dived for home. Drummond went in pursuit and, after firing 100 rounds, saw the fighter hit the ground about four miles from his own airfield. The third enemy fighter followed and dived twice to attack, being engaged by the rear gunner. On a third dive, Drummond turned tightly and fired 50 rounds at 50 yards range before his target dived steeply. While following it down, the enemy aircraft went into a spin and broke up in the air. Drummond subsequently was awarded the Distinguished Service Order.

The advance through Palestine slowed as supplies were brought up and rainy weather set in. The squadron settled down for a quiet period after its short but hectic campaign in which it had destroyed nine enemy aircraft and seen seven more go down apparently out of control. Two of their own fighters had made forced-landings but none was lost in action. In January 1918, the Vickers Bullets were replaced and the last Bristol Monoplane crashed on 17 January. They were replaced by S.E.5as and in February the Bristol Fighters were passed over to No. 1 Squadron, Australian Flying Corps. By the end of the month, No. 111 had one flight of seven Nieuport 17 Scouts and two flights equipped with 10 S.E.5as.

As Julis was nearly 30 miles from the front line, the Nieuports were moved forward to Sarona on 2 March where they could use their fast climbing advantage to intercept enemy reconnaissance aircraft as they appeared over the lines. On 27 March, Captain Drummond took off in Nieuport B3597 when a Rumpler was reported spotting by wireless-telegraphy. Climbing rapidly, Drummond spotted an enemy two-seater being attacked by Lieutenant Walker who was already on patrol. He dived and turned beneath it, firing a drum from his wing-mounted Lewis gun at close range from a 'blind' position where the enemy gunner could not reach him. Both Nieuports followed the two-seater down but at 1,500 feet, six Albatros D.IIIs appeared and dived on them. As the leader opened fire, Drummond made an '*Immelmann* turn' and got under his tail. After 50 rounds had been fired, the enemy fighter dived into a hill. His companions continued the attack and after 15 minutes the gyrating Nieuport was down to 80 feet and was fired on from the ground. By what appears to have been mutual consent, the combatants returned to about 1,000 feet, probably because the ground gunners were loosing off at any aircraft within range. Drummond found little chance to fire as he evaded the combined attacks but managed to fire half a drum into one enemy which spun away and did not return. The remaining four forced the Nieuport down again until it spun at 200 feet and flattened out with only feet to spare. At this point the engine stopped.

No sooner had the wheels touched ground than the engine burst into life again so Drummond headed for home at an altitude of five feet. The enemy fighters suddenly realised—after the Nieuport had covered about half-a-mile—that it was still flying and chased after it. For the next ten miles, the engine was running for five seconds at a time and then cutting out with a loud and disconcerting bang. This resulted in four momentary landings, one of them beside a camp full of Germans having breakfast. On this occasion, the engine fired just in time and Drummond hauled the Nieuport over a hedge and made off trailing a clothes line which it had captured while passing between two tents. Three times the enemy fighters tried to head him off but on each occasion Drummond managed to zig-zag out of their fire. Three of them flew off when the front line was crossed but the fourth refused to give up and for three minutes Nieuport and Albatros chased each other in a tight circle round a tree. At last a burst from the Lewis hit the enemy fighter which sheered off and Drummond headed for home. Finding a hill ahead that his eccentric engine could not hope to cope with, he put the Nieuport down and walked the rest of the way. The Albatros also landed near some troops but took off again before they could reach it.

A few days earlier, Captain A. H. Peck DSO, MC, was patrolling over Jericho in his S.E.5a (B52) when he saw anti-aircraft fire. The targets were two reconnaissance aircraft escorted by five fighters. Peck attacked the highest Albatros with both his fixed Vickers machine-gun and the wing-mounted Lewis and the enemy fighter turned over on its back and went down upside down. Getting on the tail of a second fighter, the same result was seen. The two-seaters were diving for home but the fast S.E.5a caught up with one of them and fired from short range. The engine began to smoke and it spun down into cloud.

Between April and June 1918, 17 enemy aircraft were destroyed for the loss of two pilots missing (and subsequently found to have been killed) and one taken prisoner. Then on 11 June Lieutenant Gledhill's Nieuport was hit by an anti-aircraft shell which removed the engine cowling and impaled it on the tail. This caused the aircraft to spin violently but fortunately the vibration dislodged the cowling and Gledhill was able to recover and crash-land unhurt inside his own lines.

Major Stent was posted back to England on 9 July and in his place arrived Major Hereward de Havilland, younger brother of Geoffrey de Havilland whose D.H.2 scouts had equipped the squadron when it first formed. Operations changed considerably after his coming as attacks on ground targets now became common. Twenty-pound Cooper bombs were fitted on racks under the wings, four being carried. At the same time, the Nieuports were replaced by more S.E.5as which became the sole equipment of the squadron.

The command of the squadron changed again on 16 September when de Havilland was admitted to hospital seriously ill and one of No. 111's flight commanders, Captain S. H. Long, took over. Preparations for another offensive were under way and a continuous patrol was maintained over the major enemy airfield at Jenin on the Lebanese border. Each aircraft dropped bombs and machine-gunned buildings during their patrols to keep the enemy air force grounded. Almost no aircraft took off during the period of the attack and when cavalry occupied Jenin they found eight new Pfalz fighters destroyed.

The S.E.s were in the air continuously harrying the retreating Turkish troops. In the narrow valleys attacks with bombs and machine-guns dispersed the enemy and by the time they emerged on to the plains there was little cohesion left in the Turkish formations. Most were rounded up by cavalry in a completely demoralised condition, never before having had to endure this form of attack. In the absence of enemy air opposition, every operational squadron was involved

in low-level strafing and the retirement turned into a rout. It was the first occasion that an army had been routed by air power.

The cavalry advance moved so fast that No. 111 was left behind. Its airfield at Ramleh was so far from the fluid front line that no further operational flights were made after 24 September when 116 bombs were dropped and 12,400 rounds of ammunition expended on the enemy troops. On 1 October, Damascus was captured and there was no further need for fighter squadrons. No. 111 moved to Kantara on the Suez Canal on 20 October and the aircraft were dismantled and packed for transfer to another front. On 30 October Turkey signed an armistice and on 11 November the First World War ended.

During its active service, the squadron destroyed 44 enemy aircraft and sent another 13 down out of control for the loss of two pilots killed, one taken prisoner and three wounded. Four more were killed in accidents and six injured. Awards consisted of four DSOs, eight MCs, two DFCs, one MM and five MSMs. A total of 4,555 hours was flown.

No. 111 returned to Ramleh on 6 February 1919, and re-equipped with Bristol Fighters which it flew over Palestine for a year before being renumbered 14 Squadron on 1 February 1920. Its short career in the Middle East had started from a nucleus provided by No. 14 so it was appropriate that it should revert to this number in the immediate post-war Royal Air Force.

First with the Hurricane

With the end of the First World War, the first-line strength of the R.A.F. dwindled to a handful of squadrons. The fighter defence of the United Kingdom was virtually non-existent for several years and its rebuilding was a slow process. Shortage of funds was symbolized by the reforming of No. 111 Squadron with only one flight in place of the normal three. On 1 October 1923, the squadron began to assemble at Duxford, Cambridgeshire with a few Gloucestershire Grebes, an early product of the famous Gloster works. It was about 20 m.p.h. faster than the wartime S.E.5a because of its 400 h.p. Armstrong Siddeley Jaguar radial engine but in most respects was little more advanced. On 1 April 1924, a second flight was formed

1 Siskin III J7163 displays No. 111's traditional black bar along its fuselage. (*Photo: Ministry of Defence H.1577.*)

2 Refuelling Gauntlets from a three-point refueller which came into service in the mid-Thirties. (*Photo: Flight International 13135.*)

1

3

2

1 Gauntlet K5267 prepares for take-off at dusk. The Squadron badge is carried on the fin and the fuselage serial has been ousted by No. 111's black bar. (*Photo: Flight International 13138.*)

2 An early formation of Hurricanes in 1938; serial numbers are carried under both wings. (*Photo: Flight International 15590.*)

3 The first squadron to receive Hurricanes, No. 111 lost their bar marking but mounted the squadron badge on the fin in the absence of a fin flash. (*Photo: Flight International 15586.*)

and equipped with the wartime Sopwith Snipe. Finally, when the third flight was formed in January 1925, Armstrong Whitworth Siskins were received and the squadron mechanics had to cope with three separate types. Fortunately, enough Siskins were available to replace the Snipe and the Grebes and became No. 111's standard equipment.

The squadron's Siskins were the subject of much experimentation in tactics and equipment. Fitted with supercharged Jaguars, they carried out trials of heated clothing, oxygen apparatus, instruments and the behaviour of pilots and engines at high altitude. In addition to its operational and experimental tasks the squadron also undertook *ab initio* training of pilots with Avro 504Ks, a chore which fortunately did not last long.

In January 1931, the first Bristol Bulldog was collected and during the following month the Siskins were transferred to No. 19 Squadron. The enhanced performance of the Bulldog—and its radio equipment—improved its effectiveness as a fighter and exercises developed all aspects of the defences of London, then assumed to be the only major target of an enemy air force.

During May and June 1936, the squadron re-equipped with Gloster Gauntlets, yet another twin-gun biplane but capable of 230 m.p.h. The transition from Gauntlet to monoplane Hawker Hurricane in January 1938 was a major step. The top speed jumped by nearly 100 m.p.h., the armament from two to eight machine-guns and, additionally, enclosed cockpits and retractable undercarriages were also new to most pilots.

No. 111 lost no time in publicising the fact that they were the first, and sole, Hurricane squadron. To Northolt (Middlesex) came a procession of visitors to see the new fighters in their unaccustomed camouflage. A startled British public learned that on 10 February 1938, the Commanding Officer, Squadron Leader J. W. Gillan, flew from Edinburgh to Northolt at an average speed of 408 m.p.h. (helped by a less-publicised but energetic tail wind).

When war with Germany broke out on 3 September 1939, the squadron dispersed its aircraft and its 22 pilots braced themselves to meet the expected fleets of bombers bent on the destruction of London. None came but a heavy toll was taken of runaway barrage balloons. With the Netherlands neutral, enemy bombers faced a roundabout route to get to S.E. England and most of their activity was around the north of the British Isles. So No. 111 was sent to Acklington in Northumberland on 27 October to join Nos. 152 and 607 Squadrons.

It was a month before an enemy aircraft was caught. Squadron Leader Harry Broadhurst—destined to reach high rank in the R.A.F.—was flying N2340 when he sighted a Heinkel He 111 medium bomber eight miles east of Alnwick as it emerged from a bank of cloud. Climbing into the cloud he emerged to find the Heinkel immediately above him. As the Hurricane approached, it was spotted by the German crew. The bomber dived for cloud cover 1,500 feet below firing its ventral gun. Broadhurst got directly behind the Heinkel's tail and fired long bursts whereupon it turned on its side and dived vertically into cloud with smoke trailing. The Hurricane had to pull out violently to avoid hitting the water, a manoeuvre the Heinkel was then in no position to emulate. No. 111 chalked up its first victim of the war.

On 13 May 1940 the squadron returned to Northolt as German armoured divisions roared through France and the Low Countries. 'B' Flight was detached to Kenley (Surrey) to join a flight of No. 253 Squadron as a composite squadron under the command of Squadron Leader J. M. Thompson. To get closer to the places it was defending, Vitry-en-Artois (near Douai) was used as an advanced base. On 17 May, a patrol over Cambrai found and disposed of a Henschel Hs 126 observation monoplane, returned to Vitry to refuel and on taking off again was attacked by 14 Messerschmitt Bf 109s while getting airborne. Flight Lieutenant Darwood (in L2051) was shot down as the other Hurricanes evaded the attack. Later in the day, a further patrol took off to intercept enemy aircraft over Douai and accounted for four enemy aircraft. As the Hurricanes landed to refuel again, Vitry was attacked by seven Dornier Do 17s which rendered almost all the 20 aircraft on the airfield unserviceable.

'A' Flight had, in the meantime, flown to Lille/Marcq to escort bombers and tangled with nine Bf 110s. Flying Officer H. M. Ferris raked one and saw the crew bale out while Sergeant W. L. Dymond spotted a Do 17 on the way back and sent it diving into the ground.

After a week at Digby (Lincolnshire) to recover from their intensive operations, the squadron was recalled to North Weald (Essex) to help cover the evacuation beaches of Dunkirk. On 31 May, the first such patrol claimed five Bf 109s and two He 111s. By the end of June, all Northern France was in German hands and the *Luftwaffe* was ranged to attack England.

For the first part of the Battle of Britain, No. 111 was based on the famous former civil airport at Croydon (Surrey) where it was heavily engaged in repelling waves of enemy bombers. On 15 August it became the target of enemy bombs when 15 Bf 110s attacked Croydon in error for the nearby fighter station at Kenley. Nine of No. 111's Hurricanes had just taken off when bombs wrecked many of the airport buildings. Five were shot down by the squadron without loss and No. 32 squadron accounted for two more, the commander of the crack *Erprobungsgruppe 210*, *Hauptmann* Walter Rubensdorfer, being shot down near Rotherfield (Sussex) by Squadron Leader Thompson.

Four days later, the squadron was withdrawn to Debden (Essex) for rest, returning to Croydon on 3 September for five days—losing two pilots next day in a dogfight over Folkestone (Kent) in which two Bf 109s were shot down. On 8 September, No. 111 moved to Drem near Edinburgh to refit, its total claims to date amounting to 94 enemy aircraft destroyed, plus 18 probables, for the loss of 15 pilots.

Training new pilots was then the main preoccupation until the end of 1940 and few enemy aircraft were found. In April 1941 conversion to Spitfires took place and in July the squadron moved south again. By now the *Luftwaffe* was firmly on the defensive and fighter squadrons were ranging over Northern France seeking out the Messerschmitts and Focke-Wulfs, as well as escorting bombers. Pairs of fighters undertook low-level sweeps in search of 'targets of opportunity'. In November the squadron was transferred to night-flying but the policy of using single-engined fighters for night fighting was changing and No. 111 returned to daylight operations again. 'Sweeps', escorts and intruder missions followed one after the other until September 1942 when a move was made to Fowlmere, near Duxford (Cambridgeshire) and tropical kit was issued. Obviously something was afoot but nobody would say where the squadron was going.

In Mediterranean Skies

Since the capitulation in June 1940, France had been divided into two opposing camps. The Free French under Charles de Gaulle continued to fight the Germans on every front while the new government which had signed the armistice governed Southern France and most of its colonies from the temporary capital at Vichy. The main preoccupation of the latter was to avoid upsetting the Germans and thus preserve part of France from enemy occupation. In so doing, they came into conflict with the hard-pressed Allies, notably in North Africa which flanked the long hazardous run through the Western Mediterranean to Malta.

Allied strategy required the clearance of the North African shores to enable the Mediterranean to be opened to shipping and an assault on Italy prepared. The Eighth Army in Egypt was ready to take the offensive and push the German and Italian armies out of Libya but it was probable that the enemy would merely retreat into Tunisia and that the Vichy government would do nothing to stop them. In order to trap

1

1 Hawker Hurricane I L1555—one of the first delivered to No. 111 Squadron in January 1938—was the ninth production aircraft and remained with the squadron until transferred to No. 6 Operational Training Unit (later No. 56 O.T.U.) in June 1940. It suffered engine failure on 2 February 1941, was damaged in a resultant forced landing and was not repaired.

2 Vickers F.B.19 A5223 carried a roundel edged in white low on the fuselage side and had a mispainted serial for a time, F.B.19 serials starting at A5225.

3 Armstrong Whitworth III J7002 served with No. 111 Squadron in 1926. It was later used at No. 3 Flying Training School and ended its career on 25 April 1933, when it crashed into a hangar at Grantham while taking-off and was destroyed by fire.

2

3

1

1 English Electric Lightning F.1A XM215 carried the most elaborate colour scheme used by No. 111 Squadron before Ministry policy decreed more discreet markings for fighter squadrons. It later passed to No. 226 Operational Conversion Unit when 'Treble-One' received Lightning F.3s.

2 Sopwith Snipe F2527 was built in 1918 and was stored until issued to No. 111 Squadron in 1924. The Snipe was the earliest type to carry the squadron's black bar marking.

3 Gloster Meteor F.8 WK693 served with No. 111 Squadron in 1954 and carried its first post-war markings fore and aft of the fuselage roundels.

2

3

1

2

3

1 A line-up of Hurricanes at Northolt after the Munich crisis had brought code letters to R.A.F. aircraft. 'TM. was used until the outbreak of World War Two. (*Photo: Air-Britain archives.*)

2 Spitfire VB EP166 was named 'O Bandeirante' and replaced BM634 which originally carried the name and was presented to the R.A.F. by the State of Sao Paulo, Brazil in June 1942. Standing beside it is Squadron Leader Peter Wickham, No. 111's Commanding Officer. (*Photo: I.W.M. CH.6826.*)

3 A Spitfire IX lands at No. 111's airstrip at Lago, Italy after a patrol over the Anzio beachhead in early 1944. (*Photo: I.W.M. CNA.2436.*)

4 A 'Black Arrow' Hunter F.6 (XG194) flies over Frensham Ponds, Surrey on a sortie from Farnborough. (*Photo: Ministry of Defence PRB.15661.*)

5 The black markings of No. 111 Squadron reappeared when it reformed with Meteor F.8s in December 1953. (*Photo: Ministry of Defence H.1316.*)

the Axis forces, a series of landings in North Africa was planned with American troops landing in Morocco and British in Algeria.

To provide air cover for the British landings, large numbers of Spitfires were assembled at Gibraltar ready to be flown to Algeria when airfields were captured. No. 111's pilots were sent by sea, arriving on 6 November to find Gibraltar's airfield crammed with Spitfires being assembled. On November 8, the Allied invasion force surged ashore and French resistance crumbled in a few days enabling the Spitfires to depart for their new base at the Algiers civil airport of Maison Blanche on 11 November. German bombers attacked every night and by day patrols were flown to protect the numerous ships bringing troops and supplies. On 22 November, one of these brought No. 111's ground crews who moved east to join the squadron's pilots at Bone.

The weather was not what those who regarded North Africa as being the Sahara Desert had expected. It rained interminably and the airfields were soggy morasses for much of the time. The weather, too, had prevented the Army reaching Tunis before the Germans but by early 1943 the Eighth Army had reached Southern Tunisia and the enemy was penned between Allied armies and the sea. Besides the two British armies, there was an American and a French corps in the line and all required air cover from the fighter squadrons. German fighters made hit-and-run attacks on airfields from their dry bases on the Tunis plain and were, in turn, bombed by medium- and heavy-bombers escorted by strong fighter forces.

By April, the scene was set for the last act. The German defence line was broken and Allied troops rolled down from the hills to Tunis and Bizerte. With the Royal Navy patrolling the sea routes to Sicily and Italy, there were few attempts at evacuation by sea but large formations of German transport aircraft evacuated key personnel during the last days. Many were shot down and on 1 May, Wing Commander Gilroy led the squadron on a sweep over the Gulf of Tunis. North of Bizerte, an He 111 escorted by Bf 109s was shot down after the escort had made off. A second patrol in the afternoon found 15 Bf 110s and eight Bf 109s flying at low level towards the Tunisian coast, presumably to provide escort for a convoy of transport aircraft. The squadron attacked and destroyed six Bf 110s and a Bf 109 at the cost of one Spitfire damaged by a cannon shell.

Enemy resistance collapsed and on 13 May the squadron moved into Protville airfield near Tunis amid the wreckage of German aircraft. It was not to be a long stay as the next assault was already under way. Early in June, the Spitfires took-off for Malta and on 15 June

4

5

began flying 'sweeps' over Sicily where the next blow was to fall. A flight of Spitfire IXs was added to supplement the Mark VCs. Soon after the landings, No. 111 moved to Comiso airfield which had just been captured and spent most of its time escorting Curtiss Kittyhawk fighter-bombers before providing air cover for the landings at Salerno on 9 September. A tenuous beachhead had been secured, German reaction being greater than expected as Italy had surrendered and it was presumed that the Germans would pull back to a defence line further north. Rough airstrips had been levelled and the squadron moved into one of them. Suspicions that not everything had gone according to plan were aroused by the fact that artillery was firing at the enemy from the wrong side of the airstrip. The front line appeared to be too close for comfort. Fortunately, a breakout was achieved, the front line moved forward a safe distance and Naples fell, enabling the squadron to move to a permanent airfield outside the city.

Few enemy aircraft were now seen but in May 1944 the 200th enemy aircraft was destroyed. As the Army moved forward, so the squadron changed its base to keep within range of the front line over which it maintained constant patrols. In June, Rome was captured and in July No. 111 was transferred to Corsica.

An Allied landing in Southern France was scheduled for August and the northern end of Corsica was pockmarked with airfields for the covering fighters. The squadron arrived at Calvi on 20 July and began escorting bombers over Southern France. Strong patrols were sent to protect the invasion beaches and on 20 August the first of No. 111's Spitfires landed on the improvised airstrip at Ramatuelle. Moving north, the squadron reached Lyon on 7 September, attacking enemy troops retreating to Germany wherever found. Though operating within range of home-based aircraft, No. 111 was not to be lost to the Italian campaign and, early in October, it was recalled to Italy.

Since few enemy aircraft appeared over Italy, most of the fighter squadrons were fitted with bomb racks and sent out to attack enemy communications, barracks and vehicles. No. 111 was no exception and a rack for a 500-lb bomb was fitted under the fuselage. For the rest of the war, the squadron's fighter-bombers ranged over Northern Italy until, on 3 May 1945 the German forces in Italy surrendered.

On 16 May, a move was made to Klagenfurt in Southern Austria where the squadron remained as part of the occupation forces until disbanded on 12 May 1947.

No. 111 Squadron reformed on 2 December 1953 at North Weald and received Meteor F.8s. Eighteen months flying these twin-jet fighters paved the way for the advent of Hawker Hunters in June 1955. To mark the occasion, a repeat performance of the famous Hurricane flight from Edinburgh to London was planned. On 8 August 1955, Squadron Leader Roger Topp flew WT739 over the same route at an average speed of 717.5 m.p.h.

In 1957, the squadron was nominated as Fighter Command's aerobatic team. In carrying out its task, No. 111 brought the art of formation aerobatics to a state never equalled with operational aircraft. A display routine using nine Hunters was developed and, combined with smoke generators, the aerobatics in formation overshadowed every other aerobatic team in the world. The Hunters were painted in No. 111's traditional black and were immediately dubbed 'The Black Arrows' by the national press. The combination of showmanship and first-class flying was attained without detriment to the operational role of the squadron in contrast to the specialized display teams from other countries.

The nine-Hunter formation was revealed at the 1957 S.B.A.C. Farnborough Show where it appeared in place of the expected 5-plane team. The effect was not gained without sundry alarms. One modification to the routine came when the 'Big Nine' diamond formation carried out a bomb-burst at the beginning of its display, the reason being an Auster which had chosen that moment to potter across the airfield. Another practice session brought out the local fire-brigade in search of what had been reported as a large bomber crashing, which the pilots took as a compliment to their close station-keeping.

The unexpected can always happen—and usually does at precisely the worst moment. Topp was leading the squadron for a display in front of the television cameras when his radio went dead. Unable to hear or be heard, he found himself flying the sequences by watching the other aircraft. Realizing what had happened, the deputy leader, Flight Lieutenant George Aird, had begun to call the changes to which the leader conformed. It is doubtful if anyone on the ground ever realized that the normal polished performance was any different from its predecessors.

For the 1958 Farnborough Display, the squadron planned another surprise. With assistance from No. 56 Squadron, it arrived on the scene with no fewer than 22 Hunters which it proceeded to loop and roll in formation. Any doubts as to 'Treble One's' leadership in formation aerobatics were shattered on the spot.

Squadron Leader Peter Latham took over later in the year and for the next two seasons the nine-plane team polished its routines to perfection. There were visits to displays in Europe and the squadron achieved international fame. At the end of the 1960 season, display flying came to an end as, early in 1961, No. 111 was scheduled to re-equip with English Electric Lightnings.

The Lightnings began to arrive in April 1961 and the squadron bade farewell to its beloved Hunters. Twice the speed did not make up for the flying qualities of the Hunter. Engine power appeared to have taken over from aerodynamics and the Lightnings were ugly. But with a pair of powerful Avon engines, the Lightning was an effective interceptor armed with air-to-air missiles and advanced radar equipment.

Today 'Treble One' flies its black-flashed Lightning F.3s from Wattisham (Suffolk) over the same countryside traversed by its Siskins 45 years before. Its motto 'Adstantes' means 'standing-by', the traditional role of interceptor squadrons poised to defend the British Isles ever since the threat of air attack first cast its shadow.

1 A formation of Lightning F.1As off the coast of East Anglia. (*Photo: Ministry of Defence PRB.21720.*)

2 Five Black Hunters formate over the River Alde just south of Aldeburgh, Suffolk. (*Photo: Ministry of Defence PRB.13314.*)

3 With the Lightning, No. 111 replaced its guns by missiles carried on stubs on either side of the fuselage. (*Photo: Ministry of Defence PRB.36030.*)

4 In 1961, 'Treble One' collected five types flown by the squadron for a commemorative photograph. The Spitfire is a Mk. 19 from the Battle of Britain Flight—with the addition of a black bar. From top to bottom: Lightning F.1A, Hunter F.6, Meteor F.8, Spitfire 19, Hurricane 2. (*Photo: Ministry of Defence PRB.23829.*)

5 Twenty-two Hunters loop in formation in preparation for the 1958 S.B.A.C. Display (with the assistance of 8 Hunters from No. 56 Squadron). (*Photo: Ministry of Defence PRB.15707.*)

1

2

3

4

5

SQUADRON BASES

Deir el Belah, Palestine	1 August 1917
Julis, Palestine	1 December 1917
Ramleh, Palestine	29 March 1918
Kantara, Egypt	20 October 1918
Ramleh, Palestine	6 February 1919 to 1 February 1920
Duxford, Cambridgeshire	1 October 1923
Hornchurch, Essex	1 April 1928
Northolt, Middlesex	12 July 1934
Acklington, Northumberland	27 October 1939
Drem, East Lothian	7 December 1939
Wick, Caithness	27 February 1940
Northolt, Middlesex	13 May 1940
Digby, Lincolnshire	21 May 1940
North Weald, Essex	30 May 1940
Croydon, Surrey	4 June 1940
Debden, Essex	19 August 1940
Croydon, Surrey	3 September 1940
Drem, East Lothian	8 September 1940
Dyce, Aberdeenshire	12 October 1940
Montrose, Angus (formerly Forfarshire)	Det. 12 October 1941 to 5 April 1941
North Weald, Essex	20 July 1941
Debden, Essex	1 November 1941
North Weald, Essex	15 December 1941
Debden, Essex	22 December 1941
Gravesend, Kent	30 June 1942
Debden, Essex	7 July 1942
Kenley, Surrey	28 July 1942
Martlesham Heath, Suffolk	21 September 1942
Fowlmere, Cambridgeshire	27 September 1942
Embarked for Gibraltar (Air echelon)	20 October 1942
Gibraltar (Air echelon)	6 November 1942
Maison Blanche, Algeria	11 November 1942
Bône, Algeria	14 November 1942
(Ground echelon rejoined at Bone on	30 November 1942)
Souk-el-Arba, Algeria	3 December 1942
Souk-el-Khemis, Algeria	22 December 1942
Protville I Tunisia	13 May 1943
Mateur, Tunisia	25 May 1943
Safi, Malta	10 June 1943
Comiso, Sicily	15 July 1943
Pachino South, Sicily	30 July 1943
Panebianco, Sicily	29 August 1943
Cassala, Sicily	2 September 1943
Falcone, Sicily	6 September 1943
Montecorvino, Italy	23 September 1943
Battipaglia, Italy	28 September 1943
Capodichino, Italy	11 October 1943
Lago, Italy	15 January 1944
Tre Cancelli, Italy	5 June 1944
Tarquinia, Italy	14 June 1944
Grosseto, Italy	25 June 1944
Piombino, Italy	5 July 1944
Calvi, Corsica	20 July 1944
Ramatuelle, France	20 August 1944
Sisteron, France	25 August 1944
Lyon/Bron, France	7 September 1944
La Jasse, France	26 September 1944
Peretola, Italy	2 October 1944
Rimini, Italy	13 November 1944
Ravenna, Italy	17 February 1944
Rivolto, Italy	4 May 1945
Klagenfurt, Austria	16 May 1945
Zeltweg, Austria	12 September 1945
Tissano, Italy	23 September 1946
Treviso, Italy	16 January 1947 to 12 May 1947
North Weald, Essex	2 December 1953
Wattisham, Suffolk	18 June 1958

SQUADRON EQUIPMENT
Period of Use & Typical Serial and Code Letters

Aircraft	Period of Use	Serial and Code
Bristol Scout	August 1917 to October 1917	——
Bristol M.1B	August 1917 to January 1918	A5142
D.H.2	August 1917 to December 1917	——
Vickers F.B.19	August 1917 to January 1918	A5224
Bristol F.2B	September 1917 to February 1918	A7194
S.E.5a	October 1917 to February 1919	B52
Nieuport 17	January 1918 to July 1918	B3597
Bristol F.2B	February 1919 to February 1920	E2288
Gloucestershire (Gloster) Grebe II	October 1923 to January 1925	——
Sopwith Snipe	April 1924 to January 1925	F2441
Armstrong Whitworth Siskin III	June 1924 to November 1926	J7152
Armstrong Whitworth Siskin IIIA	September 1926 to February 1931	J9193
Bristol Bulldog IIA	January 1931 to June 1936	K1683
Gloster Gauntlet II	May 1936 to February 1938	K7813
Hawker Hurricane I	January 1938 to April 1941	L1621 (TM-D)
Hawker Hurricane IIA	March 1941 to May 1941	W9117
Supermarine Spitfire I	April 1941 to May 1941	N3100
Supermarine Spitfire IIA	May 1941 to September 1941	P8428
Supermarine Spitfire VB	August 1941 to October 1942	W3450
Supermarine Spitfire VC	November 1942 to January 1944	JG925 (JU-Q)
Supermarine Spitfire IXC	June 1943 to May 1947	EN517 (JU-X)
Gloster Meteor F.8	December 1953 to June 1955	WL129 (P)
Hawker Hunter F.4	June 1955 to November 1956	WV379 (V)
Hawker Hunter F.6	November 1956 to April 1961	XF416 (T)
English Electric Lightning F.1A	April 1961 to February 1965	XM188 (F)
English Electric Lightning F.3	December 1964 to date	XR716 (F)

COMMANDING OFFICERS

Major A.Shekleton	1 August 1917
Major F.W.Stent	21 November 1917
Major H.de Havilland DSO	8 July 1918
Major S.H.Long DSO MC	15 September 1918
Major R.M.Drummond DSO MC	20 February 1919
Major C.E.H.Medhurst OBE MC	8 March 1919
S/Ldr. T.F.Hazell DSO, MC, DFC	1 December 1923
F/Lt. H.W.Woollett DSO, MC	6 February 1925
S/Ldr. G.W.Roberts MC	2 March 1925
F/Lt. A.C.Collier	14 October 1927
S/Ldr. K.R.Park MC, DFC	18 November 1927
S/Ldr. F.O.Soden DFC	8 March 1929
S/Ldr. L.H.Slatter OBE, DSC, DFC	25 October 1929
S/Ldr. E.R.Openshaw	13 November 1930
F/Lt. J.T.Paine	28 February 1933
S/Ldr. M.B.Frew DSO, MC, AFC	11 May 1933
S/Ldr. E.P.Mackay	1 August 1934
F/Lt. C.W.Weedon	18 October 1935
F/Lt. I.E.Brodie	21 December 1935
S/Ldr. G.V.Howard DFC	2 March 1936
S/Ldr. J.W.Gillan AFC	20 October 1937
S/Ldr. H.Broadhurst AFC	16 January 1939
S/Ldr. J.M.Thompson	24 January 1940
S/Ldr. A.J.Biggar	5 October 1940
S/Ldr. J.S.McLean	10 February 1941
S/Ldr. G.F.Brotchie	1 September 1941
S/Ldr. P.R.Wickham DFC	17 March 1942
S/Ldr. A.C.Bartley DFC	31 August 1942
S/Ldr. J.J.Leroux DFC	26 January 1943
S/Ldr. G.A.Hill DFC, RCAF*	30 April 1943
S/Ldr. P.G.H.Matthews DFC	19 August 1943
S/Ldr. M.S.Hards DFC, DFM	19 December 1943
S/Ldr. P.H.Humphreys DFC	7 April 1944
Major T.P.L.Murray DFC, SAAF*	19 November 1944
S/Ldr. B.F.G.Darby	28 February 1945
S/Ldr. L.W.Farrow	9 March 1945
S/Ldr. P. Cannam	26 September 1945
S/Ldr. D.F.Dennis DSO, DFC	26 June 1946
S/Ldr. R.T.Llewellyn DFM	18 January 1947
S/Ldr. H. Pears DFC	2 December 1953
S/Ldr. R.L.Topp AFC	23 January 1955
S/Ldr. P.A.Latham AFC	13 October 1958
S/Ldr. K.A.C.Wirdnam	14 November 1960
S/Ldr. G.P.Black AFC	4 January 1964
W/Cdr. D.P.Hall AFC	2 August 1966
W/Cdr. L. Swart AFC	27 May 1968
W/Cdr. P.S.Collins AFC, BA	6 July 1970

* RCAF—Royal Canadian Air Force
SAAF—South African Air Force